CRAZY CHARLIE

REVOLUTIONARY OR NEO NAZI

By Ron Chepesiuk

Published in the United States of America by Strategic Media Books, Ind., 782 Wofford St., Rock Hill, SC 29730.

www.strategicmediabooks.com

Manufactured in the United States of America.

ISBN-10:1939521386

ISBN-13:978-1-939521-38-5

Requests for permission should be directed to:
strategicmediabooks@gmail.com

or mailed to:

Permissions
Strategic Media Books, Inc.
782 Wofford St
Rock Hill, SC 29730

Distributed to the trade by:

Cardinal Publishers Group
2402 North Shadeland Ave., Suite A
Indianapolis, IN 46219

Table of Contents

PROLOGUE . . . . **iii**

CHAPTER 1 . . . . **1**
ROOTS

CHAPTER 2 . . . . **13**
GETTING EDUCATED

CHAPTER 3 . . . . **29**
PARADISE FOUND

CHAPTER 4 . . . . **45**
COMING HOME

CHAPTER 5 . . . . **63**
INDICTMENT

PHOTOS **75**

CHAPTER 6 . . . . **85**
ON THE RUN

CHAPTER 7 . . . . **101**
A FUGTIVE IN COLOMBIA

CHAPTER 8 . . . . **115**
THE TRIAL

CHAPTER 9 . . . . **131**
CRAZY CHARLIE — THE LEGEND

UPDATE **143**

ACKNOWLEDGEMENTS **149**

SELECTED BIBLIOGRAPHY **151**
BOOKS
COURT RECORDS
MAGAZINE AND NEWSPAPER ARTICLES
INTERNET ARTICLES

INDEX **159**

PROLOGUE

Drug lord Carlos Lehder was on the run, and Colonel Jaime Ramirez, head of Colombia's anti-narcotics police, was in hot pursuit. Ever since his friend and colleague, Rodrigo Lara Bonilla, Colombia's popular justice minister, was murdered on April 30, 1984, by *sicarios* - or contract killers—working for the Medlin Cartel, Ramirez had vowed to "never give up" in trying to bring Lara's murderers to justice and putting their bosses out of the drug business.

Ramirez was good to his word. In the first seven months of 1984, hundreds of drug traffickers were arrested, and the number of cocaine seizures went up eleven fold over the previous four years.

Yet trying to bring one of the big Medellín godfathers to justice was proving to be a much more difficult thing. The bad guys also seemed to know when the police were coming. Often, they would escape with food still cooking on the stove or cigarettes burning in an ashtray.

Ramirez would have liked to bring Medellín Cartel godfathers Pablo Escobar, Jorge Ochoa and Jose Gonzalo Rodriguez Gacha to justice for Lara Bonilla's murder; but for him, Carlos Lehder, the cartel's "transportation minister," became his special project and he devoted a lot his agency's resources to tracking him. Ramirez knew that after several months of hiding in Nicaragua, Lehder had returned to Colombia, making it now possible to capture him.

Ramirez's investigation of Lehder received a boost when, six days after Lara Bonilla's murder, Colombian President Belisario Betancur Cuertas signed the order for Lehder's extradition to the U.S. The drug lord's appeals were exhausted, and Ramirez knew that if he found and captured Lehder, he would face no problems in sending the drug lord to the U.S.

Ramirez had come close to capturing Lehder before. Ramirez's men missed Lehder by four days at Airpua in the Llanos, a hundred miles from Bogota. Then in November of 1984, the colonel tracked Lehder to one of the smuggling operations he was setting up near Magangué, but he was not there when Ramirez's men moved in and busted the facility.

Lehder remained defiant. He began sending letters to the media denouncing "U.S. imperialism" and he vowed that he would return to public life again. In February 1984, a startled Colombia watched as

Lehder gave an interview to Spanish television from one of his jungle hideouts. Dressed in fatigue pants and sleeveless black vest, the bearded and unkempt drug lord sat on a chair with his back to a river. Lehder looked as if he had snorted one line of cocaine too many.

Lehder's comments bordered on the paranoid. He told the television crew he was "planning to form a five-hundred-thousand-man army to defend Colombia's national sovereignty." He scoffed at the idea that Hitler killed six million Jews claiming that Germany never had more than one million Jews.

Then Lehder suddenly switched gears, going from a position that defended anticommunist Nazism to one that embraced revolutionary socialism. He attacked the U.S. as a society "guided by *Playboy* magazine" and "drunk on pornography."

Later at his office, Ramirez watched the videotape of the bizarre rendezvous in the jungle several times, focusing on Lehder's appearance and gestures rather than his comments. Carlos was losing it, the police chief concluded. He began to feel good about his prospects for catching the man that more and more Colombians knew as "Crazy Charlie." Lehder would trip up, the colonel was certain. It was just a matter of time.

☙ ❧

CHAPTER 1

ROOTS

Nothing in Carlos Lehder's early life gives any indication that he was destined to become one of history's most notorious drug lords and a man whose persona and unpredictable behavior would earn him the nickname of "Crazy Charlie." Lehder grew up in a relatively comfortable and, by Colombian standards, middle class environment, popular among classmates and peers, defiant of authority, and inquisitive of the world around him.

Lehder was born on September 7, 1947, in Armenia, a small provincial town in the mountainous region of central Colombia famous for growing the best coffee plants in the country. His father, Wilhelm, was a German engineer, who managed to immigrate to Colombia from Germany before World War II and subsequently played an important role in building the infrastructure that eventually connected the towns of rural Colombia. Cables were purportedly sent from the U.S. Embassy in Colombia describing Wilhelm Lehder as an ardent Nazi sympathizer, but nothing ever developed from this assessment.

Carlos Toro, who grew up with Lehder and then later in life joined his drug trafficking organization, says he never saw Carlos Lehder show any indication that he shared his father's sympathies, although Lehder did share his father's love of things German. Toro remembers Lehder's father as "aloof and not very friendly.... It was difficult to get close to Mr. Lehder and to communicate with him," Toro recalled. "He had few friends. He would spend much of the day by himself in a café in in the city center drinking coffee."

Wilhelm married Elizabeth Rivas, a woman about a decade his junior. Elizabeth, who grew up in Manizales, came from a humble background and possessed a strict moral code. She was primarily a homemaker who loved the social life. Physically, Wilhelm and Elena were a study in contrast. Wilhelm was tall and blond and Viking looking, as Toro remembers him. Elizabeth, on the other hand, was a former beauty queen with stunning, classic Latin good looks. Carlos Lehder, who grew up to be about 150 pounds in weight and 5'4" in height, took after his mother in physical appearance. Lehder's two brothers, Guillermo and Frederico, and his sister Elena, who had Down Syndrome, took after their father.

Carlos Toro remembers his boyhood friend as the most popular boy in their social circle. "From day one Carlos was charismatic," Toto recalled. "He was very popular, especially with the young girls. He attracted people. He was a risk taker, and I admired that quality. But, frankly, he was out of my league. He was too outgoing and I was too shy. We talked and liked each other and became friends, but we were never close."

In the rural Colombia of Carlos Lehder's youth, if a family had money they would send their children to a private school in Bogota, the nation's capital. But before the Lehders could do that the couple divorced. Carlos Lehder was then about four years old. "It wasn't really a good marriage," Toro recalled. "Soon after marrying, the Lehders began to have their problems. Wilhelm was old school; he wanted his wife to be a homemaker. Elizabeth, on the other hand, was a young woman with artistic talent who wanted more out of life. She saw that life offered more than simply taking care of children and washing diapers. Carlos had his mother's restless spirit and wanted to know about the big world out there."

Still, Elizabeth was a good mother. According to Toro, it was she who took the Lehder children to Club America, the local country club in Armenia, and to social events, taught them to play tennis, and exposed them to the world.

A legal divorce for Lehder's parents was out of the question. "Divorce was illegal in Colombia in those days, so the Lehders went to civil court and got a legal separation," Toro recalled.

Lehder took his parents' separation hard, according Toro. "He was angry at his mother for leaving the family and going out into the world on her own. He took his father's side. He was the only one of the children to do that."

After the parents split up, the mother returned to Manizales for a while and then traveled to Central America to live. Carlos would visit her often. "Carlos was very close to his mother, but he didn't like it in Central America and returned to Colombia," Toro explained.

Lehder was a rebel. At the private school in Bogota where Lehder eventually attended, he stayed out late at night and often challenged authority. He got into trouble frequently and ended up being suspended. "He amazed us kids," Fernando Mejia, a friend recalled. "Carlos was expelled from school for throwing an inkwell at the blackboard when the teacher tried to discipline him."

So, was Carlos Lehder a violent kid? After all, later in life he garnered a reputation as a killer who used violence to further his criminal objectives. Toro said he never saw this side of his former friend's personality, neither in their youth nor later in life when he worked for Lehder's drug trafficking organization.

Toro recalled the time he, his wife, and Carlos Lehder, now a powerful drug lord for the Medellín Cartel, attended a private social event. All three sat together.

"My wife was really beautiful," Toro explained. "A friend of the people who invited us had too many drinks and came over to our table to ask my wife to dance. She asked me what she should do. I told her: 'It's up to you. I trust you.' She turned the guy down. The man walked away but returned about twenty minutes later, drunker and more aggressive. He asked my wife: 'What's wrong with me?' My wife told him politely that she was with her husband. Thanks for asking but no thanks.

"The man walked away but then he returned again. This time he grabbed my wife's arm. I got up, saying to myself: 'I'm going to kill this son of a bitch.' Carlos (Lehder) tells me to wait. He orders his bodyguards to haul the guy outside to the parking lot. The body guards returned and said the son of a bitch is still acting up. Should they kill him?

"Carlos turns to me and says: 'It's up to you. Do you want him dead?' I thought about it, and then I told Carlos to let the guy live. So, yeah, I wasn't with Carlos all the time, but I don't think he was a killer."

But Crazy Charlie's personality did change, according to Toro. "I saw him both in his youth and as a drug dealer. Wealth and power changed my friend. When I saw him as a drug trafficker, he was not the down-to-earth person I knew as a kid. But he was never as bad a person as (Pablo) Escobar."

According to Toro, Lehder may not have been a model student, but he was certainly educated for a young man. "He was intelligent, read books, and followed the news," Toro said. "He was constantly reading and wanting to learn. He was way ahead of the other kids in his knowledge about the world." Later, Lehder showed his inquisitive mind in Danbury prison where he strived to learn all he could about the drug trade.

Fernando Arenas, Lehder's personal pilot, said newspapers were Lehder's obsession. "He read every single line in every single newspaper, so he was up to date with what was going on almost everywhere in the world."

Certain stories have circulated about Carlos' formative period, which, say historians and journalists who have studied Lehder's life, provide clues to his personality. Two stories come from Carlos' father. According to Wilhelm, at age eight, Carlos, all by himself, designed a water pump. "It was perfect. It would have worked," Wilhelm recalled.

Another story from the father shows Lehder's ardent desire and craving for public attention. Carlos once wrote to a Hollywood film company announcing his intention to become an actor. "We always asked if he would go to Hollywood to be an actor," Wilhelm said.

Later in his life Lehder became notorious for his bisexuality, drug use, and political rhetoric, but Toro said, "In our youth, I never saw any evidence that Carlos was bisexual, nor did he exhibit any kind of rabid anti-Americanism. Of course, this was the 1950s and '60s, and we didn't know what cocaine was and we weren't using marijuana."

Was Lehder anti-Semitic? Toro said he never saw any signs during Lehder's formative years that he was anti-Semitic. "In Colombia in those days, there was no such thing as racism," Toro said. "Race was not an issue and skin color was not really a problem with Colombians."

Toro added that he would have loved to have been a "fly on the wall" in the Lehder household so he could learn further the Lehder view on race and Jews. "I know Carlos loved his Germanic roots. He talked about going to Germany to meet his father's family. His dad must have played a big role in Carlos' coming to admire Adolph Hitler. But we never talked about Hitler. In fact, the only time I really talked with Carlos about Hitler was in his last days of freedom before he was captured and extradited to the U.S."

Sometime in 1965, Toro ran into Lehder in downtown Armenia. It was a time when Lehder was about to experience a major change in his life. "Carlos says to me, 'Guess what I have in my pocket?'" Toro recalled. "He showed me the page from his Colombian passport containing his visa to the U.S. In those days, an American visa to the U.S. was very easy to get. Carlos told me he had dropped out of school and was going to live with his brother, Frederico, in Michigan." Frederico, who became an architect, had moved to the U.S. in 1962 to continue his education. He was later drafted into the U.S. Army and sent to Vietnam.

Lehder was about eighteen years old when he left for the U.S. He would later say that he lived in the U.S. "half like a hippy," learning to love the Beatles' music and to speak fluent English. Later, reports described how Lehder, a capable pilot, supposedly flew drug-smuggling missions into Florida while passionately singing along to Beatles' cassettes in the cockpit. Both Jung and Toro dismiss the idea that Lehder flew planes. Still, such colorful anecdotes and Lehder's unabashed willingness to take risks contributed to the legend of Crazy Charlie

It is rumored that Lehder married an American woman and that the couple separated. Friends of Lehder would say that they did not know her name or whereabouts.

As records show, Lehder did marry a Cuban beauty named Yemel Nacel whom he had met in Montreal, Canada, on a 1977 business trip. Yemel provided Lehder with a New York State driver's license she had stolen from a former schoolmate named Joe Leon. Lehder used the license to travel to Canada.

Thereafter, Lehder became known to many people as "Joe Lehder."

Nacel later recalled, "I was just a college student at City College of New York. He was a waiter in Long Island at Carl Hoppi German Restaurant (now the Westbury Manor). But he was always doing a little better, like importing and exporting cars....That was our honeymoon."

The Lehders moved to Miami where they rented a condominium at the Ocean Pavilion on Collins Drive. It was there that Lehder started his drug smuggling empire.

Meanwhile, the Lehder-Nacel marriage did not get off to a great start. George Jung, who later became Lehder's partner in drug trade, recalled, "After Lehder married Yemel, he told me he wanted me to live with him and Mel in Miami. I told him: 'You just got married. I don't want to live with you guys.' But he insisted, so I rented a penthouse in Miami."

According to Jung, the marriage was a disaster. "Mel didn't know how to cook. She burned everything. Carlos would go nuts, and she would go to the balcony and cry. Lehder would go out after her, pissed. It was chaos. But, it really got bad after Mel told Carlos she had slept with women. I had to keep from laughing, but Carlos went crazy again. I got out of there. I didn't need a domestic dispute that would attract the police. In 1984, Lehder told Yemel that in 1981 he had divorced her in Haiti."

Interestingly, no record of that divorce exists. After his marriage to Yemel, it is believed Lehder married Lilianna Garcia Osirio, a pretty woman from his hometown of Armenia, but that, too, is a mystery since no record of the marriage can be found. Lilliana said her daughter was evidence of the marriage.

Yemel claimed that it was impossible for Lehder to have children because he had an unusually low sperm count. Given the bizarre stories about his marital status, Lehder was "earning" his moniker of "Crazy Charlie."

It was also reported that Lehder was sexually abused while living with relatives in Detroit, hence an explanation of how Lehder became bi-sexual. This story, too, is unsubstantiated.

Lehder lived in New York City for a while where one source remembered him as a pot dealer. "I would see him in the bars (where) we hung out," the source recalled. "He seemed kind of wild, but a nice guy. He was struggling to get by like the rest of us, but with one big difference: Lehder was an illegal immigrant."

As Lehder struggled to make his criminal mark on the world, he adopted multiple identities, using, among other monikers, Joe Lemon, Joe Leather, Carlos Lipher, Roselio Cessinica, Roselio de Grullaid, Ruben Montes, Carlos Enrique, Rivas Carlos and Rivas Enrique. Later, at Norman's Cay in the Bahamas, Lehder would tell people to call him "Joe." He would go into a monologue about Joe Kennedy and Prohibition. Lehder would say: "He (Kennedy) dealt in booze; I deal in coke. What's the difference, brother?"

Lehder also made the dubious claim that he was once a member of Uncle Sam's Peace Corps, which President John F. Kennedy created, and that the Peace Corps had encouraged Colombian *campesinos* to cultivate the coca plant commercially.

By the early 1970s, Lehder had begun to acquire an extensive rap sheet. He was busted in Mineola, New York, and charged with an unauthorized use of a motor vehicle. FBI agents in New Haven, Connecticut, were investigating Lehder on suspicion that he was transporting stolen vehicles to South America. By now, Lehder was traveling frequently back and forth between the U.S., Canada, and South America.

Acting on an FBI warrant, the U.S. Border Patrol arrested Lehder on January 9, 1973, as he crossed from Windsor, Canada, through the Detroit tunnel. He was released on a $25,000 bond, but he did not appear in court to answer the charges. Lehder was also convicted of drug possession in September 1973.

All of these arrests, along with the frustrating realization that he was a failure as a criminal, most likely contributed to his bitter hatred of Uncle Sam. He would come to the conclusion that narcotics were a powerful weapon that could be used against the U.S.

to destroy it. At Lehder's trial in Jacksonville, Florida, in 1987, George Jung testified that Lehder hoped that flooding the country with cocaine could disrupt the American political system.

By 1973, Lehder had little to show from his life of crime. Indeed, he was on his way to prison, serving his time at the Danbury Correctional Institute. There he would get an education on how the drug trade worked, something that transformed his life.

☙ ❧

CHAPTER 2

GETTING EDUCATED

Carlos Lehder was in his mid-20s when incarcerated for the first time in the Federal Correctional Institution, a low-level security prison in Danbury, Massachusetts. At this point in his life, Lehder had done nothing to distinguish himself in what looked like his chosen occupation in life: criminality. In fact, he could best be described as a loser.

Historically, the Danbury prison had accommodated several high-profile prisoners. For instance, poet Robert Lowell spent nine months there in the early 1940s after refusing to enter the draft. Screenwriter Ring Lardner, Jr., also served nine months at Danbury after refusing to answer questions about whether he was a member of the Communist Party USA.

Fellow inmates at Danbury included G. Gordon Liddy of Watergate fame; Clifford Irving, the Howard Hughes hoax biographer; and the Berrigan brothers, Dan and Phil, peace activists from the Vietnam anti-war movement and Johnny Semple, the New York Jets defensive back, who had helped the Jets win the 1969 Super Bowl, was there for cashing some $15,000 in stolen U.S Treasury checks.

Many among the notorious inmate population had expertise in crime. As Bruce Porter, Jung's biographer explained, the inmate population was "the tenured faculty of a school for scoundrels." George Jung would say that Lehder entered Danbury with a bachelor's degree in marijuana smuggling and left with a doctorate in cocaine smuggling.

Lehder shared a jail cell with George Jung, then a part-time marijuana dealer who had acquired a vast amount of knowledge and experience about drug smuggling. Jung later recalled, "Danbury was a very unique and interesting place. It was mellow and laid back. I knew many interesting people in Danbury, from bankers to lawyers to doctors to Indian chiefs. You could, more or less, learn anything you wanted to learn in there in reference to illegal activity."

George Jung would have a dramatic impact on Carlos Lehder's life. Jung was born on August 6, 1942, in Boston, Massachusetts, but was raised in Weymouth, Massachusetts. In high school, he was a poor student but an outstanding football player. After high school graduation, Jung attended the University of Southern Mississippi where he studied advertising. Jung never graduated, but he had begun using marijuana and selling small amounts of it.

Jung, along with his best buddy, "Tuna," headed to California where the hippy scene was starting. At the time, it seemed everybody in California was in the drug trafficking business, either as consumers or as retailers, and Jung became a heavy user of marijuana and LSD. Both Jung and Tuna were unemployed, so Tuna suggested they make money-selling marijuana. Jung was soon impressed by the money he and his friend were making. The two friends could buy marijuana for $60 a kilo and sell it for about $300.

In the book *Blow*, the biography about Jung's life, which was later made into a movie starring Johnny Depp, Jung described his philosophy of being a drug dealer: "The way I see it, being in the drug business was like being an executive in any business. If you wanted to climb the ladder, you sought out people and pursued those who were better and bigger than you were, and you tried to ingratiate yourself. Then you find out they are not as big as you thought they were, and so you go beyond them, and before you know it, they're working for you. Anyway, that's the way I wanted it to work."

After moving to California, Jung met the man who changed his life: a well-connected 5'2" U.S. Marine-turned hairdresser named Richard Barile. Jung was soon getting all his pot he wanted through Barile. Jung started out using a flight attendant girlfriend to transport drugs in suitcases on the flights she made; but to make more money; he expanded his operation to fly the drugs in from Puerta Vallarta, Mexico, using professional pilots and airplanes stolen from private airports in Cape Cod. Jung chose Puerta Vallarta because he had seen a movie titled "Night of the Iguana" which had been filmed there, starring Richard Burton and Elizabeth Taylor.

Jung bought the marijuana for $20 a kilo in Mexico and sold it for between $300 and $350 a kilo in the U.S. By this time, the summer of 1968, George's California friends were calling him "Boston George." Jung became a pot star, and, as Jung saw it, he was simply "supplying a need that everybody my age wanted."

The drug game ended for Jung when he was arrested in Chicago for carrying a truckload of marijuana. At the time, Jung was staying at the Playboy Club, and the drug connection he had in the city was also involved in the heroin business. "I had no idea he was moving heroin," Jung recalled. "Of course, to save himself, he snitched on me and they arrested me for pot smuggling. They told me: 'We're sorry. We really don't want to bust pot people but this is tied into a heroin operation, and we have to arrest you.' I would never have involved myself. I thought heroin was evil and pot okay."

Jung's lawyers earned their pay by getting Jung a light sentence. He would have to serve no more than twelve months in prison. The year was 1974.

Cellmates Lehder and Jung developed a close relationship. Jung remembers Lehder as being mellow, well mannered, and neat in appearance. "Carlos said he was from Colombia and he spoke excellent English," Jung explained. "I was pretty lucky to have him as a cellmate. As time went on, we got to know each other. One day he asked me if I knew anything about cocaine. I told him, 'No, I have no idea.' I asked, 'How much does it cost?' He said from $4,000 to $5,000 a kilo. Immediately bells started to go off, and the cash register started ringing in my head."

From then on, Lehder and Jung began an intense ongoing discussion about all things cocaine and the best ways to smuggle the illicit drug into the U.S. Jung was seven years Lehder's senior, and he had a lot of experience transporting marijuana, but he knew very little about cocaine. It was understandable. America was still four or five years away from the cocaine explosion that would plague the country.

Cocaine, a powerful drug contained in the leaves of the coca shrub, is a plant grown primarily in the South American countries of Peru, Bolivia, and Colombia. In the 1960s, cocaine was viewed as "the champagne of drugs," meaning it was the drug of choice for the rich and famous. In 1974, the National Institute of Drug Abuse reported five million Americans had used cocaine at least once. Ten years later, that number had jumped to twenty-two million.

Lehder explained to Jung why cocaine was a much better drug to smuggle than marijuana. For one thing, cocaine was less bulky. For another, it was much more profitable. Lehder predicted that cocaine would be the drug of the future that traffickers like themselves would smuggle.

Lehder bragged that he had unlimited access to large amounts of cocaine in Colombia. Jung admitted he didn't know much about cocaine, but he did have a distribution network in place in Los Angeles that could supply well-off drug users in the film and recording industries.

Cocaine was not the only topic of conversation. Often, they would turn to politics. Both Jung and Lehder were radicals in their own way. Lehder once described cocaine as an atomic bomb that could destroy the U.S. from within. As Guy Gugliotta and Jeff Leen described their conversations in *The Kings of Cocaine,* "Lehder dreamed of running his own country. He talked constantly of revolution, and he revered Ernesto 'Che' Guevara, the (Cuban) matinee idol of the revolutionary left. Lehder also admired John Lennon and Adolph Hitler. Jung, a son of Woodstock nation whose own tastes ran to Bob Dylan, could understand Che and Lennon, but Hitler was too much."

Today, Jung says, "Carlos was talking to the wrong man when it came to Hitler, but actually his pro-Nazism didn't really come out until he was out of prison."

According to Jung, once Lehder found out who he was and what he knew about the illegal drug trade, Lehder began following him around so he could learn all he could. He had an unquenchable thirst for knowledge. "Carlos didn't know what longitude and latitude were when he came to Danbury," Jung recalled. "Me and some of the boys taught him about navigation. He studied maps with us."

Lehder was aggressive in his desire to learn all he could, but he could have been more aggressive at Danbury protecting his turf. "One time we were in the weight room, and Carlos got into a disagreement with an inmate," Jung recalled. "The inmate slapped Carlos' face, but Carlos didn't do anything. I told Carlos it was dangerous to put up with that kind of shit in the pen. You have to try to hit the other guy back. Carlos really didn't exhibit any aggressive behavior while we were at Danbury."

Jung was not the only inmate from whom Lehder learned. Inmate Dan Moore, for example, was the former president of the Surety Bank and Trust Company of Wakefield, Massachusetts, who had absconded with $8.1 million of his institution's assets. In return for Spanish lessons, Moore taught Lehder about the banking system and how it worked and how to launder money to offshore accounts. Lehder not only listened, but he copied the valuable information down on notepads and filed them away under the appropriate subject.

While at Danbury, Lehder modeled his dress and manner after the tough-talking Watergate conspirator G. Gordon Liddy who had helped organize and direct the burglary of Democratic National Committee headquarters in Washington, DC's Watergate building in May and June of 1972. Liddy was convicted of burglary, conspiracy and refusing to testify to the U.S. Senate Committee investigating Watergate. He would spend nearly fifty-two months in federal prisons, including time in Danbury.

In Jung's biography, *Blow,* Jung recalled how Lehder "watched Liddy and began imitating him—keeping carefully groomed, his cloths crisp, strutting around the yard with his file of information under his arm."

In the spring of 1975, when Jung was paroled, he gave Lehder his parents' address and told him to get in touch after Lehder was out of prison and back in Colombia. Four months later, Lehder was released, but because he was an illegal alien, he was deported to Colombia. He now began working on the plan that would make him rich and notorious.

Meanwhile, George Jung was floundering as he tried to re-establish himself in life. Then one day in February 1975 he received a telegram from Auto Lehder, a car dealership in the Colombian city of Medellín that

Lehder was using as a front for his criminal activities. It read:

> THE WEATHER IS BEAUTIFUL. PLEASE COME DOWN.
>
> SIGNED: YOUR FRIEND CARLOS.

Jung was still on parole, and he did not want to take the chance of leaving the country and something going wrong. So he sent his old friend Frank Shea instead. Shea met with Lehder at a ranch, and the two hit it off. Shea called Jung to tell him that they had hit the jackpot. Cocaine was going to make them rich.

The plan Lehder devised was to smuggle about fifteen kilos of cocaine into the U.S., which in 1976 was worth about $750,000. Jung decided to use two female couriers, Betsy Strautman and Winny Polly. On the promise of an all-expense paid vacation, the two women would fly the drugs from the island of Antigua to Boston. In Antiqua, Strautman and Polly met with Lehder and some of his associates.

The plan went smoothly and the two couriers returned to Boston with the cocaine, carrying it in the false bottoms of their suitcases. The first run made $235,000 for Jung. Business became so good that Jung was able to sell fifty kilos in two weeks at a profit of $2.2 million. But it was small change compared to what the future promised.

Remarkably, Lehder had no problem about whom he used as couriers to get his illicit drugs to the market. "I was in California and I had just transferred a lot of coke," Jung recalled. "Lehder called me and said he was sending somebody to me who would bring some cocaine in a couple of suitcases. 'You can sell it for me,' Carlos said. In those days you could smuggle coke on airplanes using a couple of suitcases.

"Carlos said, 'You'll be surprised who I'm sending.' I said, 'I don't like surprises when it comes to business. Who is it?' He laughed and said, 'you'll see.'

"The next day, guess who knocks on my door carrying a couple of suitcases filled with cocaine? Carlos' mother! She told me she wanted a vacation, so Carlos told her she could come out to sunny California and he would pay. All she had to do was transport some cocaine for him. I couldn't believe it! I called Carlos and told him, 'You fucking scumbag. You're sick!'"

The use of mules or couriers to smuggle cocaine was a success, but Lehder's goal was to traffic cocaine in bulk by private airplane. Lehder had many plans for politics, but he needed a lot of money to finance his ambitions.

Lehder had hoped Frank Shea would be the pilot he needed to fly his private plane, but Shea was upset with his cut of the drug profits and dropped out. A friend set Lehder up with Barry Kane, a Massachusetts attorney who owned a private plane. Jung asked Kane if he wanted to help smuggle cocaine from South America.

Kane did not hesitate to join Jung's venture. Lehder, Jung, and Kane met in Toronto, Canada, to discuss their business arrangement. Lehder said he knew a drug dealer named Pablo Escobar who owned a ranch outside Medellín. They could use the ranch to ship what Kane figured would be about 300 kilos a trip using his plane. There would be no problems because Escobar would pay off the authorities to leave the plane alone.

Kane said he had connections in the Bahamas and would be able to use the islands for fueling his plane on the way to and from Colombia. Lehder wanted to do the smuggling through Mexico, but the new plan seemed perfect. There was a problem, though. Lehder did not have the money to get the plan off the ground. So Lehder and Jung planned another trip in which a woman with suitcases would go on a drug smuggling mission and meet Lehder in Venezuela. Lehder, however, never showed up. On October 19, 1976, he was arrested for smuggling Chevrolet station wagons into Colombia.

Lehder was sent to Bella Vista, a new prison in Medellín, where he met an American named Stephen Yakovac, a one-time auto mechanic and computer repairman who would later play a role helping Lehder to realize his drug smuggling ambitions. Lehder and Yakovac became friends and passed their days smoking marijuana, playing monopoly and gabbing. Lehder talked about his plan for a worldwide network of cocaine smugglers linked by his transportation pipeline, which would be based in the Bahamas.

Lehder spent just two months in Bella Vista, and when the time came to leave, Lehder gave Yakovac his contact information. Yakovac, however, believed he would never see his new friend again.

Lehder's drug trafficking dream became a reality when he and Jung met Barry Kane in Miami in the first week of August 1977. On the first smuggling trip from the U.S. to Escobar's ranch and back, Kane's plane carried 250 kilos of cocaine, five times as much as Carlos had ever handled. The plan went smoothly, and Lehder and Jung split a cool million dollars. Lehder now began to make plans to move his operation to the Bahamas, which would be strategically located between Colombia, the cocaine source country, and the U.S., the world's biggest illegal drug market.

But all was not going well with the Lehder-Jung partnership. Jung felt Lehder was going behind his back and dealing with his connection in California, who had hooked him up to the cocaine users in Hollywood. Jung had given in to Lehder's constant pressure to give up the contact's name.

Jung arranged a meeting with Lehder in Nassau, Bahamas, where Lehder was checking out the possible purchase of Norman's Cay, the Bahamian island located about 200 miles southeast of Miami. At the meeting, Lehder denied any backstabbing on his part, but Jung sensed that Carlos was lying.

"I went to the Bahamas with the intention of exterminating Lehder," Jung recalled. "I decided against it, but I told him, "Fuck you. You're a scumbag! He didn't say anything to me. That was the last time I saw him."

For Jung, Lehder had turned into a power-obsessed megalomaniac who had forgotten those who had helped him up the criminal ladder. Lehder broke with Jung and told him to go work for an associate in New York City. Instead, Jung, now bent on revenge, went looking for someone to kill his former partner. Jung, however, found out Lehder was now untouchable, so he called off the hit.

Jung was not the only associate with whom Lehder cut ties. Steve Yakovac joined Lehder's organization after he got out of jail. On June 11, 1978, Lehder showed up unexpectedly.

Yakovac described the meeting in his dairy: "I couldn't speak. My jaws opened and my mind whirled. It had been almost a year, a year and a half since we've spoken, and I had just about given up seeing him again. See him again I did. What a trip. We spoke a little of old times, new times and problems. In one fell swoop, he eliminated our present money dilemma with a gift of 10,000 pesos, and he lifted my spirits incredibly by telling me of his success."

A month later, upon Yakovac's release, Lehder sent a chauffeur to pick him up. "Let's go to work. Let's become millionaires," Lehder told his friend. Lehder took the Rolex off his wrist and gave it to Yakovac.

Yakovac had various jobs on Norman's Cay. He would fly as protection on cocaine loads to the U.S. once a month and was paid $5,000 per trip. In seven flights in 1978, Yakovac helped smuggle nearly one and a half tons of cocaine into the U.S. On the return trip to Norman's Cay, Yakovac brought money, which on one occasion amounted to $1.3 million.

But the good thing did not last for Yakovac. He had the temerity to question the wisdom of some of Lehder's orders, and he, too, was told to hit the road...at the point of a gun. Seduced by money and power, Lehder was now acting like a führer.

Lehder's increasing use of cocaine, no doubt, was also contributing to his erratic and volatile behavior. He was smoking cocaine base, the most addictive form of the drug.

Lehder's drug use "boosted his megalomania into the stratosphere," Gugliotta and Leen write in the *The Kings of Cocaine*. He began to affect a regal, reckless air. His obsession with power increased, as did his fascination with things German, particularly Hitler. Cocaine fed his most grandiose dreams."

Carlos Toro joined Lehder on the island as a kind of PR assistant and diplomat who, because he spoke several languages, would accompany his boss when he went abroad to Cuba, Nicaragua and other countries on business. "When I came on the island to join Carlos, I began to see a different Carlos Lehder," explained Toro. "Carlos had changed. It was quite unsettling. One now had to be careful around him."

Lehder was not satisfied with being one of the richest men from Colombia. He wanted to rule the country. In his spare time, he began studying a book titled *How to Speak in Public* as preparation for his plan to become President of Colombia.

As Lehder cut his ties, he focused his attention on Norman's Cay. Crazy Charlie was about to revolutionize the Latin American drug trade.

☙ ❧

CHAPTER 3

PARADISE FOUND

Picturesque Norman's Cay in the Bahamas is located about fifty miles from Nassau, the capitol, and twenty miles southeast of Miami. Named after an English pirate, the island was developed in the early 1970s as a popular anchorage for visiting yachts and a playground for the rich—that is, until Lehder showed up and decided to stay. There was a small residential community with a clubhouse and marina, one telephone, and electricity that came from diesel-fueled generators.

In *Cocaine Wars,* Paul Eddy and his co-authors describe what life was like for the few residents of Norman's Cay before Lehder arrived on the scene: "It was a civilized retreat for wealthy people. The Island sold excellent wine, and the restaurant at the Norman's Cay Yacht Club and Hotel served an elegant dinner, insisting that gentlemen wear jackets.

Every evening a cistern truck would rumble up and down the island's only road spraying pesticides to keep the mosquitoes at bay."

Despite its isolated location, Norman's Cay had been a busy transit point for marijuana and cocaine shipments since the late 1960s. Indeed it was a good place to be a crook, given that the Bahamas' bank secrecy laws favored criminals with a lot of dirty money to launder. The Bahamas, moreover, was run by a progressive government that was not the most cooperative of nations for the U.S.

Lehder was well aware of Norman's Cay strategic advantages and concluded that it would be an ideal transit point from which to begin the big expansion of the Latin American drug trade. In 1978 Lehder used a Guardian Trust Company in Nassau to set up a company called International Dutch Resources Ltd. for the purpose of using it to buy land in Norman's Cay. Pablo Escobar and Jorge Ochoa also opened up bank accounts in Nassau, which Lehder used to deposit the money he made from cocaine sales. Lehder could then wire-transfer the money to bank accounts in Panama.

At the time, George Jung, Lehder's partner, didn't think it was a good idea to settle in Norman's Cay. "Norman's Cay was like a red light for law enforcement," Jung recalled. "Here we are. Come and get us. I told Carlos that it was not the way to smuggle drugs. We should just keep moving instead of using one island. I thought Mexico offered a better route, but Carlos disagreed."

For a couple of million dollars in cash, the drug lord ended up purchasing a sizable portion of Norman's Cay. According to Carlos Toro, Lehder's boyhood friend and associate, "Lehder had the charisma to convince people on the island and Colombia and other surrounding neighbors to give him what he needed: refueling opportunities, the protection of the people as they unloaded cocaine, the needed refuge overnight, and so much more."

Lehder's first purchase on Norman's Cay involved a deal with Charles Beckwith, the owner of a Florida amusement park. One day, Lehder showed up at Beckwith's house unannounced with a briefcase containing $190,000 in cash. Beckwith reportedly took the cash and left the cay on the same day.

Lehder next purchased two large tracts of land located at both ends of island. The purchase at the south end included a marina, a yacht club, motel and, what was of vital importance, a well-paved airstrip about 3,500 feet in length. In order to safeguard his purchase, Lehder employed armed guards and used attack dogs. Guy Gugliotta and Jeff Leen, the authors of *Kings of Cocaine*, described how Lehder protected his investment: "People had counted as many as twenty Doberman Pinscher guard dogs in pens near the airstrip. Blond men with German accents and black satchels patrolled in Toyota jeeps and

Volkswagen vans. When boats got too close to the island, a helicopter sometimes hovered overhead. A sophisticated communications tower went up on Norman's Cay and navigational aides were installed for night time landings."

Meanwhile, Lehder did his best to intimidate the locales, forcing them to leave Norman's Cay or to rent their properties to his employees. Lehder told one of his subordinates to discourage visitors to the island by leaving "a bad taste in their mouth" so they wouldn't come back. Lehder was brazen in his efforts to control Norman's Cay, even once threatening a prominent former member of the Bahamian parliament at gunpoint on the beach at Norman's Cay.

One of the most famous visitors that Lehder chased away from Norman's Cay was Walter Cronkite, the CBC news anchor who was once called "the most trusted man in America." An avid yachtsman, Cronkite came to Norman's Cay in 1978, but to the newsman's surprise, he found the harbor empty. When Cronkite dropped anchor to investigate, a man on the pier yelled: "You can't dock here and you can't anchor out here." Cronkite sailed away.

Richard Novak, a professor who had leased a leasing business on the island, tried to fight back and alert the authorities about what was going on, but it was futile. Novak would later write a book about his experience on Norman's Cay titled *Turning the Tide: One Man against the Medellín Cartel.* Novak informed the DEA of Lehder's criminal activities on Norman's Cay, but the planes filled with cocaine still kept flying to the U.S.

Novak managed to leave the island, but one retired couple was not so lucky. In July 1980, their yacht was found drifting off Norman's Cay. On board, a corpse and blood stains. MayCay Beeler, who wrote Jack Reed's biography, *Buccaneer: The Provocative Odyssey of Jack Reed, Adventurer, Drug Smuggler and Pilot Extraordinaire,* says there is another side to the story of Lehder's residency on Norman's Cay. "In researching my book, I talked to several residents of Norman's Cay or their descendants. They said they found Lehder to be outgoing and friendly, and they told me he did a lot to help residents on the island," she explained. "Lehder actually flew some of the residents to New England for visits or wherever else they wanted to go. As to acts of violence Lehder was accused of perpetrating on the island, my sources attributed that to Lehder's German head of security, who was often out of control."

Ed Ward, an ex-U.S. Marine and marijuana smuggler who came to Norman's Cay two years before Lehder did, was one of the few locals to stay. One day in early 1978 Ward went over to see Lehder and tell him that he knew Lehder was a drug trafficker like himself, but not to worry. There was plenty of room for both of them on the island. A couple of months later, Lehder asked Ward if he wanted to smuggle cocaine for him. There was much more money to made doing that than in smuggling marijuana, Lehder told Ward. Lehder and Ward came to an agreement in which Ward would make ten smuggling trips of 25 kilos a trip for $400,000 a load.

The pilot, Jack Reed, became rich as Lehder's right hand man, flying many loads to the U.S. for him. According to Beeler, Reed was very close to Lehder. "Both Jack and Carlos were charismatic, but they had different personalities," she explained. "Lehder was extroverted and Jack, introverted. It was a nice balance that worked well for their relationship."

George Jung said Lehder would hire top-notch pilots like Ward and Reed, but then wouldn't pay them what they were worth. "Carlos thought he was paying them too much money," Jung explained. "Lehder was making millions, but he was just paying them a few hundred thousand per trip. I told Carlos: 'You think these pilots are going to be loyal to you if something goes wrong? Don't be cheap.' Carlos didn't listen to me and guess what happened? When Ed Ward went down, he became one of the biggest snitches against Carlos."

Eventually, Lehder became notorious on the island for the wild parties and orgies he had at his residence where, according to several reports, men and women had sex, switched partners, drank to oblivion, smoked marijuana and snorted cocaine. Toro recalled his first visit to the island: "I remember specifically getting out of their plane. The plane hadn't even stopped taxing on the runway, and this Land Rover pulls up and who is driving the Rover? A very beautiful naked woman, and she's coming to welcome me. So when you open the door to the plane and you find this beautiful naked lady, you say, wow! This is the place to be."

Norman's Cay became the nexus in Lehder's drug smuggling operation, and, through the use of small aircraft, the island allowed the drug lord to revolutionize the drug trade. Previously, as we have seen, Lehder and other drug dealers relied on so-called human mules who used suitcases to smuggle the drugs on regular commercial flights. Lehder's criminal genius was to devise a system that allowed him to move much larger quantities of cocaine with less risk of interdiction.

Fernando Arenas, the personal pilot for Carlos Lehder, assessed for PBS's "Frontline" program Lehder's importance to the Latin American drug trade's development: "Carlos played a very special role in establishing the (drug) business in the United States because he had Norman's Cay. He was the key person who readily expanded the Medellín Cartel's view of the business. He was the one who really had the idea of being able to move the thousands and thousands of kilos to the States."

In another "Frontline" interview, Jorge Ochoa acknowledged the importance of Norman's Cay to the drug trafficking business. "Norman's Cay was a bridge used by everyone in the business. At the time, it was something that helped me, and it helped many people.... It was almost as if law enforcement hardly existed at this point in time. It was easy to buy an island in the Bahamas. Everybody used the routes that Carlos had."

Ochoa was a founding member of the Medellín Cartel which used Norman's Cay to become the world's most powerful drug trafficking organization. The Medellín Cartel was named after the picturesque Colombian city of Medellín. Historically, Medellín had a reputation as being a smuggling center for liquor and cigarettes from the United States, and stereos, radios and television sets from the many ports in the Panama Canal Zone. Medellín began to play an important role in the international drug trade in 1973 after Chilean President Salvador Allende had either jailed or deported from Chile numerous drug traffickers who had made Chile the center of the emerging Latin America cocaine trade. The traffickers then moved to Colombia where criminals like Pablo Escobar and Fabio Ochoa, Sr., the father of the Ochoa brothers, were eager to expand the cocaine distribution network.

Lehder knew that other individuals who joined with him to form the Medellín Cartel—Pablo Escobar, Jose Gonzalo Rodriguez Gacha and the three Ochoa brothers (Jorge, Fabio and Juan David)—needed him if they were to succeed in the cocaine trade. Lehder had the system that could get their illicit product to the U.S.

Lehder became a vital part of a conglomerate of like-minded gangsters and budding drug kingpins. Pablo Escobar, the cartel's leader, was born on December 1, 1949, the son of a night watchman and school teacher, in Rionegro, Colombia, a town twenty-five miles from Medellín. Escobar often portrayed himself as coming from a poor background; in reality, his life was middle class (by Colombian standards). Interestingly, Escobar was a high school graduate, no small feat for someone of Escobar's background.

In the early 1970s, Escobar worked as a thief and bodyguard who made a quick $100,000 on the side by kidnapping and ransoming a business executive. By the late 1970s, as the cocaine trade began booming in response to American demand, Escobar was smuggling about thirty-five tons of cocaine annually out of Colombia, thanks to Lehder's transportation network.

Fabio Ochoa, Sr., helped to form the Medellín Cartel, but it was his three sons who helped make the cartel the world's most powerful drug trafficking organization. Jorge Luis, the oldest son, was most responsible for transforming his family's business into a modern drug trafficking organization. In the early 1980s, the DEA office in Bogota reported that Ochoa had become "one of the most powerful drug traffickers in Medellín and the northern coast of Colombia and is continuing to introduce one hundred to two hundred kilos of cocaine into the U.S. by several unknown methods."

Fabio, the second oldest son lived for a time in Miami during the 1970s where he headed the Ochoa family's drug distribution network. Juan David, the third Ochoa brother, owned a horse ranch in Florida and several prize *Caballos de Paso* (walking horses).

Jose Gonzalo Rodriguez Gacha was known as *El Mexicano* (The Mexican) for his love of all things Mexican. Born in 1947 in Pacho in central Colombia, the future drug kingpin ran away from home at age ten to lead a life of street crime. It is believed he joined Pablo Escobar in drug trafficking about 1976. Rodriguez Gacha was one of the Medellín Cartel's most violent members.

At the height of its power, the Medellín Cartel controlled about 80 percent of the cocaine smuggled into the U.S., according to DEA estimates. Lehder played the key role in making the Medellín Cartel the world's most powerful drug trafficking organization from the mid-1970s to the late 1980s, until, that is, it was taken down by the massive manhunt that got Pablo Escobar, the so-called "world's greatest outlaw."

It was Lehder's fast, cheap transportation system that allowed the Medellín Cartel to expand their operation and stay ahead of the competition. But according to sources, Lehder's relationship with the other Medellín Cartel founders was a marriage of convenience. "When Escobar met Lehder, I don't think Pablo particularly liked him," Toro explained. "Carlos was not from Medellín, and he was too loud and flashy for Pablo's taste. But when he started to collaborate with Carlos, he saw that Carlos could deliver the cocaine loads he put together for shipment to the U.S." Lehder truly had the transportation network in place that could make the world snow.

Lehder established the Medellín Cartel's monopoly of the Latin American drug trade by retaining a fleet of small cargo planes and high-speed boats that eliminated the middleman or "mule" who had traditionally smuggled cocaine into the United States. Under Lehder's direction, the cartel established routine air corridors in South and Central America and fuel stops in the islands of the Caribbean and Mexico. Transit sites included the Bahamas, Turks, Caico Islands, Jamaica, Mexico, and Nicaragua, which were protected by cartel employees or independent organizations, including those headed by local government officials.

The planes blended in with the traffic over the Florida Keys, and upon reaching their destination, they either dropped their drug cargos to waiting boats or landed at clandestine airstrips in Florida, Georgia or Alabama. Lehder directed the transportation network from his command post at Norman's Cay. Once safely in the U.S., cocaine shipments were taken to warehouses or stash houses and then distributed and sold to the cartel's clients.

The drug load came with a shipping manifest and a bill of lading, just as any legitimate shipping company would prepare. The names of the recipients of the cocaine were coded. In fact, no specific names were given. "We'd call one of the recipients and say 'a shipment is here,'" Toro explained. "He'd tell us where to bring it. How he got it to his destination was his problem."

For a big "service" fee based on weight of the shipment, independent dealers not affiliated with the Medellín Cartel could use the transportation system to get their drugs to the United States. Gilberto Rodriguez Orejuela, a founding member of the Cali Cartel, used his boyhood friendship with Jorge Luis Ochoa to ship an undetermined amount of cocaine through the system to Florida where he would hire trucks to ship the cocaine to the Cali Cartel's prime market, New York City.

Lehder made millions of dollars smuggling drugs, and he needed some place to hide or launder the money. The man who helped him do it was Robert Vesco. Shortly after the Bahamas gained independence in July 1973, Robert Vesco, a man that *Forbes* magazine described as "America's most famous rascal," settled there.

The former engineering school drop-out and financial wheeler-dealer had fled the U.S. in 1972 with whatever he had left from the $224 million he bilked from investors of International Overseas Services (IOS). Vesco was also accused of secretly diverting $20,000 to Richard Nixon's presidential campaign as part of a scheme to deflect a corruption probe by the U.S.'s Securities and Exchange Commission. Vesco developed close ties with the Lynden Pindling's Bahamian-led government, and while based in Norman's Cay, he operated like a man who knew he would not be extradited.

In October 1978, Vesco purchased for $180,000 a deserted island lying some ten miles south of Norman's Cay called Cistern Cay. The island had no airstrip, so the only way to get there from Nassau, the Bahamian capitol, was to fly to Norman's Cay and continue on by boat.

By 1980, Vesco's money was running out and he turned to drug trafficking. Vesco's contacts in the drug trade included Carlos Lehder, and the financial swindler became a frequent visitor to Lehder's Norman's Cay in the early 1980s. The U.S. Justice Department and the DEA became convinced that they had become partners in the drug trade.

Jung says that Lehder viewed Vesco as a financial genius, and he got Vesco to help him learn how to use off shore banks to launder his millions. While testifying at General Manuel Noriega's trial in 1991, Lehder acknowledged on the witness stand that "Robert Vesco was one of my partners in the Bahamas." According to Jung, "Vesco took a lot of Lehder's money and screwed him over."

Lehder would drop a bombshell when he claimed that Vesco had introduced him to Fidel Castro. According to a 1989 U.S. government indictment filed against Vesco, Lehder sent an emissary to Cuba in the fall of 1984 to arrange a meeting with Vesco. The emissary sought Vesco's help in persuading the Castro regime to allow Lehder to fly his cocaine flights over Cuba from Colombia in route to his base in the Bahamas. A few days later, Vesco told the emissary that he had obtained Castro's permission for the over flight of Cuba.

By that time, Vesco had set himself up in comfortable exile in Cuba at a beachfront villa. The swindler owned two private jets, half a dozen cars, two yachts and a speedboat.

The Bahamian authorities knew what was going on at Norman's Cay, but turned a blind eye. It is believed that Bahamian Prime Minster Lynden Pindling was on Lehder's payroll and took huge amounts of money from the drug lord. One DEA informant said that Lehder's lawyer, Nigel Bowe, would come to Norman's Cay on the 22nd of each month, allegedly to pick up bribe money for Pindling.

Later, a Bahamian Royal Commission of Inquiry concluded that "the Prime Minister's expenditures over the years had far exceeded his income." Lehder would eventually boast that he gave hundreds of thousands of dollars in bribes to Pindling's political party.

Pindling vehemently denied the allegations and even went on NBC television in the U.S. to make an aggressive denial. Eventually, Pindling resigned from public life because of scandal, but his public image did not suffer greatly. Consider that in 2006 the Nassau International Airport was re-named Lynden Pindling International Airport in his honor.

It was inevitable that Lehder's high profile presence in Norman's Cay would attract the attention of U.S. officials. As early as November 1978, the DEA had learned of what was happening on Norman's Cay and requested and received permission from the Bahamian government the authorization to conduct a thirty-day undercover operation on the island.

Toro said the DEA was Lehder's greatest fear, and he never understood why the agency didn't move aggressively to put their drug ring out of business. "We expected them at any moment to swoop in and bust us," Toro explained. "We had all kinds of contingency plans in anticipation they would crack down, but they never did."

Beeler believes the DEA could have shut down Norman's Cay at any time, if they really wanted to. "They could have simply pressured the Bahamian government to blow up the runways," she said.

The Bahamian police put Lehder under surveillance for a long time, but nothing happened. Then in September 1979, the Bahamian authorities finally raided Norman's Cay as part of Operation Raccoon. The operation involved more than thirty members of the Royal Bahamian Defense and Police Forces.

In all, Bahamian officials arrested thirty people, including Lehder who was arrested after fleeing Norman's Cay by motor boat prior to the raid. Lehder was allowed to go free, and all of Lehder's associates were released on $2,000 bail each. Only one person was convicted as a result of Operation Raccoon, and that was for carrying an unregistered gun. It is believed Lehder had once again bribed Bahamian authorities.

Soon it was business as usual on Norman's Cay. Bahamian officials conducted more raids on the island in 1980 and 1981, but Lehder was always tipped off and evaded arrest, although several of his associates were arrested. Lehder left the island for good in September 1981, and returned to Colombia. During the early 1980s, however, he continued to use Norman Cay's as part of his smuggling operation; despite the fact, the Bahamian authorities had put a permanent police station on the island.

☙ ❧

CHAPTER 4

COMING HOME

In September 1981, a little more than a year after acquiring Norman's Cay, Lehder left his day-to-day operations to subordinates and returned to his hometown of Armenia in Colombia. Gugliotta and Leen described Crazy Charlie's situation at the time: (Lehder) "was twice divorced, unattached, and thirty-one years old; his millions were intact and burning a hole in his pocket. He decided to invest them in his home town of Armenia where he had not lived for fifteen years."

Lehder left behind on Norman's Cay a staging post for the Medellín's smuggling operations that was just one of many such posts in Latin America. The size of the drug shipments had dictated the need for multiple routes from locations throughout Mexico and Latin America. By now, the Medellín Cartel, thanks in large part to Carlos Lehder, had a strong international operation that touched many countries, including, Bolivia, Peru, Honduras, the United States, as well as Canada and Europe, and some would say Asia.

Escobar, Lehder, and their colleagues had not appeared yet on *Forbes* magazine's list of the world's 500 richest people, but their illicit activities were making them tens of millions of dollars a day. By 1986, the Medellín Cartel controlled over 80 percent of the global cocaine market, shipping around fifteen tons of the drug to the United States daily.

Lehder was not shy about letting the world know his big plans for Armenia vowing, "I'm going to make this a real capitol, so that the entire world can visit it, and the fucking Yankees can finally appreciate what we have here."

Back in 1978, Lehder, who, by then was garnering a lot of money from the drug trade, sent a letter to the governor of Quindio province, introducing himself as the president of a company from Nassau, Bahamas, named the Air Montes Company Ltd. According to Lehder, the business was dedicated to the international buying and selling of airplanes. He further revealed that his company donated airplanes to communities who lacked air transport, and guess what? The company had chosen the province of Quindio to receive a Piper Navajo 1968 which would arrive shortly. The plane did arrive during the Christmas holiday of 1978, much to the delight of the duly impressed local townsfolk.

Upon his return to Armenia, Lehder moved quickly. He set up a parent corporation, Cebu Quindio, which launched its first development project: the building of an "alpine" resort ten miles from Armenia. The resort would cater to the "world traveler."

Lehder further revealed that he would also build a $3 million complex called *La Posada Alemana*, which would include a small zoo, gourmet restaurant, a wine bar, a discotheque named after John Lennon, one of his idols, thirty well-equipped villas and several swimming pools. Lehder commissioned a well-known Colombian sculptor, Rodrigo Arenas Bentacur, to render a statue of a naked Lennon, with a gaping bullet hole in his back. *La Posada Alemana* was opened with much fanfare and a big party that local leaders attended.

Rodrigo Arenas Bentacur was just the beginning. Lehder looked for other investment opportunities in the province by traveling about in a ten-car caravan with a silver Mercedes and a gray Porsche equipped with the latest cellular telephone equipment in pursuit of his objectives. Lehder was rich enough to keep three aircraft and two helicopters on permanent standby. He caused real estate prices in Armenia to skyrocket by literally buying up the city, condominiums, office buildings, and warehouses.

Lehder bought cattle ranches as well. One of them, the *Hacienda Pisamal*, contained about 700 acres.

Lehder's investing caused quite a stir in Quindio province. Estimates of how much money he had to invest were put at $30 million to $270 million. When asked by one childhood friend where he got his money, Lehder explained matter-of-factly, "I worked in restaurants in New York. Then I sold cars and later airplanes in the United States." Lehder would be asked that question many times during his return to Armenia and each time the answer was little bit different.

At the height of his empire, Lehder's enterprise employed 268 people, which was twice the number employed by Bavaria, the beer company which had been Armenia's biggest employer. With his high profile and evidence of power and money, Lehder became a celebrity and the media followed his every move.

Lehder started his own newspaper, *Quindio Libre*, which he distributed nationally. The paper opposed anything American and praised Carlos Lehder, its publisher. Luis Fernando Mejia, the newspaper's editor, wrote: "Lehder, a man of a new era, captain of the seas and skies, landed in Quindio, home of the Indian chiefs, warriors and poets and idealists, at a time when dark clouds hang over the Republic."

Lehder knew what good press could do for his image. So he shrewdly bought the favor of the Fourth Estate, legally, of course. He commiserated with the Colombian media about their miserable working conditions, lamenting that "it is not fair that journalists who represent the voice of reason and the flame of freedom in our democracy have to conduct their affairs in a place like this." In a well-publicized event he presented a $3000 check to the local press association's president for improvements to the association's building. When the improvements were completed, the association, in gratitude, named one of their refurbished rooms, El Salon Bahamas, in Lehder's honor.

The Roman Catholic Church was one of the beneficiaries of Lehder's largesse. Indeed, one powerful church official, Bishop Dario Castrillon, did not hide the fact that he accepted donations from Lehder. Why shouldn't they, the bishop argued, when the money went to the poor? The bishop, who later became an archbishop, even attended the opening of Lehder's entertainment complex in Quindio in mid-1983, an act which appeared by many to be signaling the bishop's blessing of the complex.

But Lehder was a man of excesses, a hedonist who could not control himself, and the locals eventually soured on their generous benefactor. The locals really didn't like the impact Lehder was having on their youth. Youngsters seemed to idolize Lehder, routinely referring to him in the street as Don Carlos. The *La Posada Alemana's* discotheque became notorious for drug use, and there were reports of naked young men and women chasing each other on the grounds at all hours of the night. Rumors abounded that as many as twenty young women from prominent local families had run away to stay with Lehder. It was also rumored that Lehder had gotten four or five of Armenia's young girls pregnant.

Local charities began turning down Lehder's donations, while Armenia's most prominent social clubs denied him admission. Lehder angrily claimed that the rejection was political. "The Armenia aristocracy doesn't want me here because I came to serve the people and not to serve them (the aristocracy)," he complained.

In retaliation, he organized his own political party: The Latin National Movement. The Latin National Movement was modeled on Hitler's National Socialist Party, and it included the equivalent of Hitler's youth auxiliary. Lehder attracted crowds of up to 10,000 people, many of whom were enticed to come by the drug lord's distribution of $5 bills at his rallies. Its platform affirmed that the people had the right to possess small amounts of marijuana and reiterated its opposition to the extradition of drug traffickers from Colombia to the U.S. "Marijuana is for the people," the Movement proclaimed.

Lehder went further and made cocaine trafficking the party's central campaign theme. Lehder declared, "Cocaine is for milking the rich." In one bizarre radio interview Lehder claimed that the profits from cocaine trade have actually been channeled towards the common people in Colombia and that's why the country's oligarchy was envious.

In other public addresses and appearances, Lehder made many bizarre comments. For instance, he claimed that Colombia's cocaine traffickers were no different than the U.S.'s prominent Kennedy family that got rich smuggling booze during Prohibition. Critics should first look at how Colombia's elite acquired their wealth before casting stones at him, Lehder argued. He claimed he was not materialistic and only interested in the welfare of Colombia, even though evidence of his greed and excesses were all around him.

Lehder did not know it but, by not being able to keep his big mouth shut, he was sowing the seeds of his own destruction. As Simon Strong, the author of *Whitewash: Pablo Escobar and Cocaine Wars,* explained. "It was Lehder's desire to be a public figure that would trigger his downfall. It meant that he carried the brunt of any offensive against the traffickers and enabled him to be made into a scapegoat—which would prove just as useful to his colleagues as it would be to the Colombian and U.S. governments."

Lehder was not the only Medellín Cartel leader with political aspirations. Pablo Escobar had them, but he was less "in your face" about it. To garner respectability, Escobar shrewdly cultivated an image as a generous benefactor. He employed an army of public relations professionals to handle his public image. He had a radio show, "Civics on the March," where he talked about all the good he was doing for the Colombian people.

Escobar projected humble roots telling one Colombian newspaper that in his high school days, he didn't have any money, "but as an active community member in my barrio, I promoted the construction of a school and the creation of a fund for indigent students."

Escobar walked the talk. He developed such construction projects as Medellín without Slums, which led to a building of a 1,000 low-income housing unit in a north Medellín landfill known as Barrio Pablo Escobar. It was a shrewd public relations gimmick that endeared Escobar to the poor people of Medellín and gave Don Pablo, as he formally became known, the status of a folk hero—a status that endears him even today.

When the authorities finally hunted down and killed Escobar in December 1993, the outpouring of grief was so great at Escobar's funeral that it had to be canceled when an emotional crowd of 5,000, pushing to get into the mortuary to see the late drug kingpin's body, shattered the window. Today, the grave of Escobar is lovingly cared for, showing that Don Pablo is still revered by many in the region, especially the poor.

In 1982, Escobar was elected to the Colombian Congress as an alternative representative from Envigado. Escobar ran on a ticket with Jairo Ortega. When Ortega was sick or had to be absent for some other reason, Escobar would substitute for him. Escobar had higher political ambitions, but he didn't count on having to deal with an intractable force named Rodrigo Lara Bonilla.

In August 1983, Colombian President Belisario Betancur appointed Rodrigo Lara Bonilla Minister of Justice. Lara Bonilla was fearless in his approach to justice, and before too long in office he was publicly denouncing the drug cartels, especially the big one from Medellín. Upon Escobar's election to the Colombian Congress, Lara Bonilla embarrassed Escobar by publicly denouncing him as a drug trafficker who had corrupted the country's politics and sports.

The politicians, drug dealers and journalists, whom Lara Bonilla threatened, tried to destroy the justice minister by falsely linking him to corruption. Jaime Ortega, Escobar's ally in Congress, presented a false check to the chamber that was supposedly for Lara Bonilla and drawn by known drug trafficker Evaristo Porras. Lara Bonilla's enemies even produced a recorded conversation between Lara Bonilla and Porras that questioned Lara Bonilla's honesty.

Lehder made sensational headlines when he attempted to walk out on the floor of the national legislature in Bogota during a debate in which Lara

Bonilla was accused of accepting drug money. President Betancur, however, stood by his justice minister, dismissing the allegations and keeping him in office.

After the link between Lara Bonilla and the drug cartels was discredited, the government began uncovering the shadowy dealings of the Medellín Cartel, specifically those of Pablo Escobar. Bonilla went further, and began to pursue criminal charges against Escobar and other drug lords.

Lara Bonilla was relentless. He ordered the seizure of hundreds of planes and properties that were allegedly used for the production and distribution of illicit drugs. Meanwhile, Escobar was forced out of office in 1984, and the U.S. canceled his visa.

Life for Carlos Lehder in Armenia was going well, that is until a November morning in 1981 when he left his *finca* in Armenia to drive ten miles to *La Posada Alemana* to check on the construction work being done. From there, Lehder headed for a nearby *finca* that he had bought and wanted to turn into a cattle ranch. Lehder felt so secure in Armenia that he never traveled with bodyguards, just his driver. A few miles from their destination, a car blocked the road. It looked as if it had stalled, and Lehder's driver stopped to help.

But it was a kidnapping. Lehder was put on the floor in the back of the car and told to stay put. Lehder, however, kicked open the door and rolled out. He got up and made a dash for safety. The kidnappers fired shots, hitting him once below the chest. The kidnappers must have thought they had killed him, for one of them said: "Let's go. The son of a bitch is gone."

Some *campesinos* found Lehder and took him to a nearby hospital. Armenia was abuzz with the word of Lehder's kidnapping. The radio station interrupted regular programming to talk about the kidnapping of the "German-Colombian investor." Crowds formed outside the hospital waiting for news of Lehder's recovery. Lehder may have been recovering in the hospital, but he had his men looking for the culprits who dared tried kidnapping him.

The drug lord recovered after two weeks, and a few days later, ten well-armed men escorted him from the hospital to his hacienda. After the kidnapping, Lehder gave up driving a car and decided he would not travel unless he had his escort of twenty-five well-armed ex-police officers with him.

Meanwhile, some 120 miles away in Medellín, kidnappers had brazenly kidnapped Marta Nieves Ochoa, the sister of the Ochoa brothers, Lehder's partners in the Medellín Cartel, from the campus of the University of Antioquia. The kidnappers were members of the M-19 guerrilla (19th of April Movement) group, which, with a membership estimated at between 1,500 and 2,000, was the second largest guerrilla group in Colombia after the Revolutionary Armed Forces of Colombia.

M-19, which took its name from the disputed Colombian election of 1970, was founded in 1974 as a group that wanted to promote revolution in Colombia. M-19's ideology was a mixture of nationalistic and populism, and it was known for carrying out a number of controversial actions, including robberies, assassinations and kidnappings.

In 1974, for instance, M-19 stole one of Simon Bolívar's swords from a museum. Five years later on New Year's Eve 1979, the group dug a tunnel into a Colombian army weapons depot, stealing more than 5,000 weapons. On February 27, 1980, M-19 stormed the Dominican Republic's Embassy and took fourteen ambassadors hostage, including one from the United States. Eventually, after tense negotiations with the Colombian government, the hostages were released and the hostage takers were allowed to leave the country for exile into Cuba.

M-19 demanded an outrageous ransom of $12 to $15 million dollars for Marta's release, but the Ochoas had no intention of paying the ransom. Instead, on December 1, 1981, they called the first ever meeting of Colombia's most prominent drug traffickers. The total number attending was about 223.

The gathering agreed to form a new group called Death to the Kidnappers (MAS) that would protect them against the guerrillas. Toro said Lehder was the mastermind behind the movement to go after the kidnappers, explaining, "They (his associates) saw he had tremendous capabilities of getting organized and doing things."

On December 13, 1981, MAS dropped fliers over Cali, an M-19 stronghold, demanding that M-19 give up Marta. The communique stated that MAS was offering a $330,000 reward leading to the capture of the kidnappers and guaranteed that those involved "will be hung from the trees in a public park or shot and marked with a sign of our group." The communique further charged that "the kidnappings had been carried out by both common criminals and subversive elements, with the latter trying to finance their activities by taking people like us, whose hard-earned money has brought progress and employment to this country, and much needed schools, hospitals, etc."

There would be no escaping the long arm of MAS, according to the communique. "Those kidnappers who are arrested by the police will be executed in prison. If their whereabouts cannot be established, our people will act on their colleagues or nearest relatives."

MAS began kidnapping the relatives of guerrilla leaders and hunting down the leaders themselves, torturing those they found. In all, ten M-19 guerrillas were kidnapped and tortured. The vigilante group went after guerrilla sympathizers as well, breaking into their homes, abusing, torturing and killing them. MAS reportedly killed or turned in to the authorities more than 100 guerrillas or their sympathizers within six weeks of the group's formation, while holding others hostage.

On February 6, 1982, MAS issued another warning: "Our patience is wearing thin." The guerrillas got the message and released the Ochoa sister. Actually, it was not as bad a deal for M-19 as it could have been. According to Paul Eddy and the authors of *Cocaine Wars*: "M-19 received money and weapons, and in return, performed chores for the traffickers: guarding their jungle strips, for example, and carrying out occasional contract killings—including at least one in Miami. The two groups had nothing in common, of course, except their mutual hatred of America."

After the historic meeting that created MAS, the drug traffickers realized that they could gain a lot through cooperation. So they called a second meeting where Colombia's leading drug lords reached agreement about how cocaine shipments would be regulated and coordinated to increase their profits and what group would control which market. Lehder and the other Medellín Cartel leaders dominated the meeting.

Then the Medellín Cartel godfathers decided to solidify their organization by creating a loose federation of drug lords headed by Escobar, Lehder, the Ochoas, and Jose Gonzalo and Rodriguez Gacha. The move reflected the cartel's growing sophistication and its status as the world's most powerful crime syndicate.

After the kidnapping of the Ochoa sister, Lehder returned to Armenia where he boasted about being an MAS member and how he had played a vital role in the group's formation. He even gave an interview to a Bogota radio station in which he acknowledged his MAS membership, stating that "kidnap victims had to protect their interests."

This did not sit well with the more low-key kingpins of the Medellín Cartel. By now, Escobar, in particular, did not have a high opinion of Crazy Charlie, despite his usefulness to the cartel, and Lehder's outspokenness confirmed his opinion of him. Indeed, in private conversation, Escobar began calling Lehder "big mouth."

Escobar and his associates were especially angered by Lehder's boast that he had donated a lot of money to presidential candidate Alphonso Michelsen and the Liberal Party. "With this indiscretion, Lehder did himself and his cartel colleagues the disservice of linking them publicly to both vigilante murder (MAS) and the Colombian political establishment," Gugliotta and Leen noted. "All the traffickers tried to buy influence but only Lehder bragged about it."

Having bought off a large part of Colombia's political establishment, the Medellín Cartel was now confident that it could expand operations without interference. So the cartel began establishing new facilities for cocaine manufacturing. Throughout late 1982 and early 1983, the cartel employed hundreds of manual workers at what became known as *Tranquilandia*. The impressive complex was located deep in the heart of the Amazon in the jungles of Caqueta and away from the reach of the Colombian authorities. *Tranquilandia* would be the biggest cocaine-manufacturing laboratory ever built, capable of manufacturing hundreds of millions of dollars worth of cocaine.

The complex employed nineteen laboratory workers. Processing supplies were flown in, and processed cocaine flown out via any one of eight airstrips constructed by the cartel for that specific purpose.

In 1983, the DEA placed satellite-tracking devices on tanks of ether (a major chemical in cocaine processing) that were purchased through the export company, Arbron Miami International Distributor Inc., from an American chemical company located in Phillipsburg, New Jersey. The DEA followed the ether shipment into the Amazon jungles and its ultimate destination, Tranquilandia.

On March 10, 1984, units of the Colombian National Police, assisted by the DEA, raided the complex. The successful operation concluded with the destruction of the complex and 13.8 metric tons of cocaine valued at $1.2 billion. The inventory the authorities confiscated was enormous: 35 drums of acetone, 482 jugs of gasoline, 363 drums of ether and 133 jugs of aviation fuel. The complex's records, moreover, showed that Tranquilandia had received 15,539 metric tons of cocaine paste and base between December 15, 1983, and February 1984.

The Colombian authorities also found a diary evidently kept by *Tranquilandia's* general manager. It contained this warning: "This is the property of Guillermo Leon Ochoa. Don't steal it, and don't pretend that it had been lost. Thank you." Police assumed that the Ochoa referenced in the diary to be related to Jorge Ochoa and his family.

In a PBS "Frontline" interview, Jorge Ochoa, Medellín Cartel kingpin, described what happened at Tranquilandia. "In 1984, the police took over Tranquilandia. A lot of people were working there... Mexican security agents arrived by air... We could have defended Tranquilandia at that moment with violence. But we said 'No, no, there should be no violence.' So police took over the place ... with no violence. They didn't fire a single bullet at anyone."

Colombian authorities later learned that Carlos was one of the managers of Tranquilandia. Somehow Crazy Charlie had managed to get away.

After the raid, U.S. and Colombian authorities realized for the first time the huge size of the Colombian drug trade. The traditional laboratory for cocaine processing had been a makeshift affair, usually set up in a suburb, most likely in Medellín, Cali and Bogota, and producing a few kilos at a time. The workers were few and equipment minimal.

Now, as Tranquilandia revealed, the Colombian drug trade required hundreds of workers, skilled chemists, pilots, a location requiring cleared forest and a landing strip for cargo planes, and many tools, generators, and communication equipment.

Carlos Lehder was largely responsible for this momentous change. He provided the transportation method by which cocaine could be mass-shipped to the market. Although illegal, drug smuggling was now the major growth industry of Latin America

While the Colombian authorities celebrated the big bust, the Medellín Cartel had no intention of licking its wounds and taking the bust in stride. Soon, the Medellín Cartel would strike back against the Colombian state, changing the entire nature of the war on drugs and, ultimately, its future direction.

CHAPTER 5

INDICTMENT

Carlo Lehder's serious problems with the law began on January 8, 1981, when he was indicted in Jacksonville, Florida. Lehder had replaced Griselda Blanco, the notorious "Black Widow," as the DEA's most wanted Colombian drug smuggler, and Uncle Sam was looking to get him in court so he could pay for his crimes.

As a DEA target, Lehder was in good company; Blanco was a Medellín Cartel founding member of the Medellín Cartel and a pioneer during the 1970s and early 1980s in moving drugs from Colombia to Miami and South Florida. The so-called Black Widow, whose criminal career was depicted in the popular documentary, *Cocaine Cowboys*, became involved in much of the gangland drug-related violence that plagued Miami during this period.

In July 1983, two U.S. federal prosecutors and a pair of DEA agents from Jacksonville, Florida, went to Colombia on a secret mission to process the case for Lehder's extradition. The U.S had a list of ten Colombians it wanted extradited to the U.S., but Uncle Sam left no doubt that Lehder was number one on the list.

Lehder was indicted along with Ed Ward, his wife, and eleven of his fellow smugglers. It was ironic that Ed Ward would be included in a drug smuggling indictment with Lehder since he had been on the outs with Crazy Charlie for some time. As he did with Jung and Yakovac, Lehder forced Ward out of his organization because he had outlived his usefulness. Lehder knew that the DEA was watching Ward, and Lehder was angry at Ward because he believed that he had been instrumental in bringing the attention of Norman's Cay to the U.S authorities. Lehder should have looked in the mirror and assessed what his high profile presence on Norman's Cay had done to attract attention.

Ward left Norman's Cay in the summer of 1980 for Haiti where he was arrested. Ward could have paid a bribe to the Haitian police and walked away, but he was tired of the corruption and decided to turn himself into the U.S. authorities. Ward was remarkably upbeat when arrested. He even shook hands with the DEA agents who took him into custody upon his arrival back to the U.S.

Ward plea bargained with the U.S. government and got a remarkably light five-year sentence. His wife received probation. In return, Ward agreed to testify against Carlos Lehder before a federal grand jury.

By now, the war on drugs had heated up, and Uncle Sam was moving to address the crisis in South Florida where a large part of the conflict was being played out. Primarily because of Lehder's successful plan to flood the U.S. with drugs, cocaine was becoming the atomic bomb that Lehder had hoped would destroy the U.S.

In 1980, James Smith, Florida's attorney general, told U.S. senators from the nation's capital that "through an accident of geography, Florida has become an internal port of entry for illicit drugs entering the U.S. We now accept the fact that the drug industry is indeed the biggest retail industry in Florida."

In 1981, authorities in Florida seized 3.5 million pounds of marijuana and 2,508 pounds of cocaine, or about two-thirds of all national seizures. Drug money, moreover, had created a surplus of $5 billion at Miami's Federal Reserve Bank, which was more than the combined holdings of the nation's twelve Federal Reserve banks.

Murder, thanks in large part to drug trafficking, had become a common event in South Florida. Indeed, the number of murders skyrocketed, going from 349 in 1979 to 569 in 1980 to 621 in 1981. So many people were being murdered in Miami that the mortuaries could not handle all the corpses. This forced the Dade County Medical Examiner's office to use refrigerated trucks to accommodate the overflow.

Drug money had corrupted all aspects of South Florida's economy, including banking, real estate and law enforcement. Economist Charles Kimball said the State of Florida was so dependent on drug money, that, if it wasn't cut off soon, Florida would experience a gigantic crisis in the real estate sector.

In November 1981, a delegation of prominent leaders from Miami calling itself Citizens against Crime went to the White House to see President Ronald Reagan and appeal for federal help in dealing with the crime epidemic wreaking havoc on South Florida. The Reagan administration responded by organizing the South Florida Task Force to coordinate efforts against the drug trafficking in South Florida.

The Reagan administration sent a veritable army of federal officials to Florida to bolster the front lines of what Uncle Sam now acknowledged was a full blown war on drugs. In its first year of operation, the South Florida Task Force claimed many victories in seizing large quantities of drugs and hauling numerous drug traffickers into court.

Uncle Sam had upped the ante in its battle against drug trafficking, but the Medellín Cartel re-adjusted and shifted the war on drugs to other parts of the country. During the 1980s and 1990s, the federal government would continue to insist that the strategy of stopping the supply of drugs from entering the country was the key to victory. It was a strategy that, ironically, made Lehder, Escobar and other Colombian drug kingpins rich and famous.

Lehder realized that extradition was the biggest problem he faced, so on March 11, 1983; he founded the *National Latin Movement*, with the sole purpose of getting rid of the 1979 U.S.-Colombia extradition treaties.

Well aware of the dangers posed by the Jacksonville indictment, Lehder had sent feelers to the U.S. State Department in 1982, offering to sell Norman's Cay to the U.S. government for $5 million if the U.S. would drop the Jacksonville case. The offer was rejected.

Uncle Sam's seriousness about extradition was seen in the Reagan administration's appointment of Lewis Tambs, ambassador to Colombia. Tambs was a tough-talking anticommunist and former national security adviser whom the Reagan administration sent to Colombia with the explicit purpose of getting the Colombian extradition treaty activated.

Despite the increasing pressure, Lehder was confident that Colombia would not approve the extradition request. Colombia nationalism and public fear of the Medellín Cartel's growing power would ensure it, he believed.

Lara Bonilla wanted Lehder extradited, but Carlos Jimenez Gomez, the Colombian attorney general, ruled that the country's extradition treaty was unconstitutional. It was a decision that Colombian President Belisario Betancur supported. Unable to resist the opportunity to embarrass the Colombian government, Lehder revealed that William Bedoya, the attorney general, had asked Lehder for $380,000, and he would make the U.S.'s extradition request go away. Bedoya was found dead from poisoning a day or so later.

The arrogant drug lord remained defiant and on the offensive. "They say I conspired against the United States," Lehder said. "I would say not only did I conspire, I will also conspire until the extradition treaty is canceled."

In September 1983, the Colombian Supreme Court ruled in favor of the U.S. on the extradition treaty, and the Justice Minister Rodrigo Lara Bonilla put out a warrant for Lehder's arrest. Lehder, however, was tipped off by someone in the justice minister's office and disappeared.

The big way that Lehder conspired was through bribes, but Justice Minister Rodrigo Lara Bonilla was a conscientious public servant who could not be bribed and who continued to pursue the investigation of the Medellín Cartel. He shocked Colombia by revealing that six of the nine teams in Colombia's professional soccer league were either partly owned or controlled by drug traffickers. He also exposed the criminal past of Medellín Cartel drug lord Pablo Escobar, who was serving as alternative delegate in the Colombian Congress. A humiliated Escobar withdrew from public life, vowing to get even with Lara Bonilla.

The last straw for the Medellín Cartel came when the Colombian authorities busted Tranquilandia. The DEA had heard that drug traffickers were sending to Colombia a major shipment of ether, a solvent like acetone that's one of the essential ingredients in cocaine production. It secretly attached radio transmitters to two of the drums in the shipment and followed the signal from Chicago to Tranquilandia. The raid caught the Medellín Cartel by surprise. Forty workers were arrested and a billion dollars' worth of cocaine was confiscated. Lehder was at Tranquilandia and barely escaped.

The Tranquilandia raid and following investigation forced the cartel to move its laboratories. Lehder helped to hide a lot of the cartel's cocaine in the small underground bunkers the cartel had hidden throughout Colombia.

Escobar was furious and he hired *sicarios* to assassinate Lara Bonilla.

The first plot to kill the justice minister came in August 1983 but fortunately for him, it was uncovered by Colombian intelligence agents before it could be executed. Lara Bonilla shrugged the plot off. Either he was too brave for his own good or else he never really understood the seriousness of the campaign to assassinate him. In one press communique, it almost seemed as if Lara Bonilla was waving a red flag in the Medellín Cartel's face when he said: "I am a dangerous minister for those who act outside the law. I only hope they don't catch me by surprise."

Representatives of the cartel met at a Colombian soda fountain to plan the details for another assassination plot on Lara Bonilla. The hit job was given to *Los Quesitos*, one of the groups of *sicarios* the Medellín Cartel employed to carry out the cartel's dirty work. The job was reportedly to be done for $521,000.

The chosen hit man would be 31-year-old Ivan Dario Guizado, an ex-convict and stone-cold killer whose lengthy rap sheet extended back in time to 1969.

It almost seemed that everybody in Colombia except Lara Bonilla knew that the Medellín Cartel would not stop until they killed him. Lewis Tambs, the U.S. ambassador to Colombia, and a U.S. DEA agent went to see Lara Bonilla to literally plead with him to take more precautions. Ambassador Tambs even reportedly offered the justice minister his bulletproof vest, but he declined.

Finally, Lara Bonilla seemed to understand the danger and agreed to the Colombian government's move to send him to Czechoslovakia to serve as Colombia's ambassador. No cartel would dare try to pull off a hit on a top government official in the communist bloc. Or at least that was the thinking. On the morning of April 30, 1984, Tambs got confirmation from the White House that Uncle Sam would hide Lara Bonilla in Texas until his appointment was cleared with the Czech government. Tambs was delighted when he heard that Lara Bonilla would take and wear his bullet proof vest.

It looked as if the Medellín Cartel's pain in the ass would escape assassination. Later, on the night of April 30, Lara Bonilla left his office in a chauffeur-driven white Mercedes Benz limousine escorted by his bodyguards. A few minutes later, the Medellín Cartel *sicario* squad caught up with their bosses' nemesis. Guizado was on a Yamaha motorcycle when he pulled out a MAC-10 from his jacket and pumped six .45-caliber bullets into Lara Bonilla; three in the head, two in the chest, one in the arm. Tambs' bulletproof vest lay in the backseat.

Lara Bonilla's escort limousine chased down Guizado. One of Lara Bonilla's bodyguards shot at the *sicario* and hit the bike's gas tank, causing the gas tank to explode and the bike to spin out of control. By then the hit man was dead from a bodyguard's bullet.

Not every leader in the Medellín Cartel approved of the hit. Lehder was one of them. He was angry, not about the killing of Lara, but because Escobar had not warned him. It was a sign that friction had developed between Lehder and Escobar. The animosity would only increase as Lehder's antics, behavior, and public statements got more bizarre and embarrassing.

The assassination outraged President Betancur. Less than five hours after the dastardly deed, the president proclaimed a state of siege in Colombia and declared a "war without quarter" against the country's drug lords. In his eulogy at Lara Bonilla's funeral, President Betancourt said: "We have reached a point where we must reflect on what is our nation, what does the word 'citizen' mean? Stop enemies of humanity! Colombia will hand over criminals wanted in other countries so they may be punished as an example." Six days later on May 8, 1984, Betancur signed the extradition order for Carlos Lehder.

Lara Bonilla was not popular among the ruling elite in Colombia for he exposed corruption in all areas of Colombian government and society. Many Colombians today, including his family, are suspicious of who was responsible for his assassination. Lara Bonilla's sister has charged that Colombia's government and the country's drug traffickers were in collusion. "The mafia itself was used by people in government," said the sister. "Rodrigo was killed because he knew too much and if he had escaped Colombia as planned he could have revealed all. Within four hours of his death, his office had been cleared of all but the most trivial of papers. It is very easy to blame everything on Pablo Escobar, but it is just too easy. His power depended on people in government."

Lara Bonilla did not escape Colombia to live another day, but Lehder and his associates in the Cali Cartel did. They were now on the run as Colombia began its biggest manhunt in history. It was a stunning counter attack against gangsters who operated like they owned the country.

During one raid in the Department of Armenia, the authorities found a letter written in December 1981 by Carlos Lehder to Jaime Michelsen Uribe, the cousin of former President Alfonso Lopez Michelsen. At the time, the cousin was president of the *Grupo Grancolombiano* banking conglomerate.

In the letter, Lehder referred to recent talks between them and wrote: "We also want to confirm our interest in *Grupo Grancolombiano* being the means for channeling our business abroad, amounting to about $20 million a year, which we would be ready to transfer to the country (Colombia) via your bank branches."

Grupo Grancolombiano soon collapsed, but one wonders what other Colombian institutions were willing to help Lehder and his associates launder their drug money. No doubt, when Lehder wrote "we", he was obviously referring to the Medellín Cartel.

After the Colombian government signed the order for Lehder's extradition to the United States, Lehder held his last press conference in Armenia, where he made a defiant proclamation. He would be extradited to the U.S. "over my dead body."

It turned out to be mere bluster. Paul Eddy and the co-authors of *Cocaine Wars* described what happened to Lehder's best-laid plans for power and greatness: "In Armenia he left behind his latest lover, his adoring well-bred girlfriends, his aircraft, his newspaper, and a pile of unpaid bills. His company collapsed and *Movimiento Latino*, the party that promised a master race, fell into disarray along with *La Posada Alemana*, and the animals in its zoo left to starve. The resort remained abandoned for a year until somebody burned most of it to the ground."

Lehder would be on the run until he had no place left to hide. He would never return to Armenia.

☙ ❧

PHOTOS

Carlos Lehder at different stages of his life.

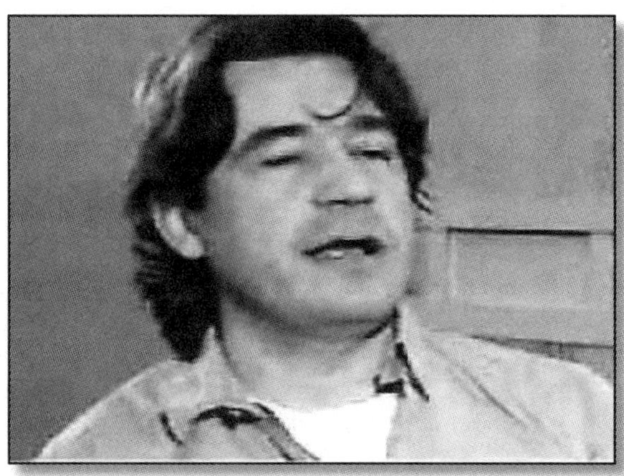

Carlos Lehder

Juan David Ochoa Vázquez

Robert Vesco

George Jung

Jack Carlton Reed

Fidel Castro

Jorge Ochoa

Fabio Ochoa

Pablo Escobar

Rodrigo Lara Bonilla

Belisario Betancur Cuartas

Carlos Toro

Jaime Ramirez

Gordon Liddy

José Gonzalo Rodríguez Gacha alias "El Mexicano"

ℵ ℶ

CHAPTER 6

ON THE RUN

Within days of signing the extradition order, Colombian authorities rounded up hundreds of suspected Medellín Cartel traffickers and threw them in jail. They seized planes, cars, trucks and other cartel property from all over Colombia.

After Brian Ross's September 5, 1983, news report on U.S. television made public the corruption of Bahamian government leaders, the Bahamian government froze all of Lehder's bank accounts and seized his property and possessions. Lehder had now lost much of his fortune, and he went from being a billionaire to a man nearly bankrupt. Lehder could not pay his help in *Posada Alemana* and they quit in mass, causing the *Posada Alemana* estate to fall into ruin.

The Medellín Cartel leaders knew Colombia was not safe once the government launched their campaign against them. Escobar and the Ochoas decided to sit out the crackdown in Panama, where the Medellín Cartel had a patron in General Manuel Noriega, the chief of the Panamanian defense forces and the country's most powerful man.

Lehder, however, would not be going with them. By this time, the Medellín Cartel leadership had essentially broken with Crazy Charlie because of his big mouth, and they now looked at Lehder more as a rival than a partner.

Lehder negotiated a deal with Nicaragua's Sandinista government that allowed him to use Nicaragua as a refuge. He eventually paid the Sandinistas millions of dollars for protection.

The Medellín Cartel had dealt with Noriega before they fled Colombia. It is believed that Noriega, when he was chief of Panama's intelligence, had helped the Jorge and Ochoa family during the Marta Nieves' kidnapping. "Noriega gave the fugitive drug lords protection and advice and listened to their complaints. Escobar alone reportedly paid Noriega $1 million in protection money.

Carlos Toro, Lehder's boyhood friend who later worked for Lehder's organization, did not have any personal contact with Manuel Noriega, but got to know his style well. "We would fly to Panama where we would meet with members of his (Noriega's) very close allies in the banking industry," Toro explained during the interview on PBS's "Frontline" television show.

"Manuel Noriega was benefiting a great deal from money laundering; even more so than from direct cocaine transportation. Manuel Noriega was always saying that he would welcome us into his country with drugs, but he never did it. He would promise that you can bring a load, but it was empty promises. He always, at the very last minute, when we were ready to bring a load and we didn't find any other sources, and we called Mr. Noriega, he'd say, 'Yes, by all means. Put the deal together, let me know what the logistics are, which coordinates, where are we going to land it, and I'll have my army take care of you.'"

Noriega was a ruthless and cunning figure who knew how to cover all his bases and play all sides. As with Saddam Hussein and other well-known dictators, Noriega had U.S. support while he proved valuable to U.S interests; and this he was. The general became a long-time valuable snitch for the CIA, feeding the agency information until 1988. Yet, when Noriega began to step out of line with U.S. interests, Uncle Sam turned against him and moved to get rid of him

But that would happen many years after the CIA had recruited Noriega while he was studying at a military academy in Peru. In 1967, Noriega received intelligence and counterintelligence training at the School of the Americas at Fort Gulick, Panama, and training in psychological operations at Fort Bragg, North Carolina.

Following a military coup in 1968 in Panama, Noriega quickly rose through the ranks of the Panamanian Defense Forces, becoming head of Panama's military intelligence and a key figure under General Omar Torrijos, the military ruler who signed a treaty with the US to restore the Panama Canal Zone to Panamanian sovereignty in 1977.

When Torrijos died in a mysterious plane crash in 1981, Noriega made his move for power. He became Panama's de facto ruler, promoting himself to full general in 1983. In November 1983, Noriega came to Washington in the manner of a head of state and visited the White House, State Department, and Pentagon, and met with CIA Director William Casey.

According to testimony before the U.S. Congress, the United States had known about Noriega's drug smuggling activities for nearly two decades, but tolerated them because he was a paid employee of the U.S. government and a valuable intelligence source. Norman Bailey, former National Security Council official, testified before Congress in 1989 that "clear and incontrovertible evidence was at least ignored, at worse hidden and denied by many different agencies and departments of the U.S. government in such a way as to provide cover and protection for Noriega's activities."

According to Gugliotta and Leen, the authors of the *Kings of Cocaine,* "Rumors of corruption, drug trafficking, gun running, and worse swirled around him (Noriega) for years, but he was able to weather every storm because the gringos felt he was the key to Panamanian political stability and the unhindered operation of the Panama Canal. He was as untouchable and well connected as any man in Latin America."

Noriega made himself especially useful to Uncle Sam by allowing the U.S. to set up listening posts in Panama and helping the U.S. campaign against the leftist Sandinista regime in Nicaragua by allowing Panama to be used as a conduit for U.S. money and weapons. The opposition to the Sandinistas was known as the Contras, the label given to the various rebel groups that were active in Nicaragua from 1979 through the early 1990s. Early on, Uncle Sam provided the Contras with financial and military support. After Congress banned that support, the Reagan administration covertly continued it.

In testifying at the trial of Manuel Noriega in 1991, Lehder described his meeting with a U.S. vice consul in Cali, Colombia, in the early 1980s. He said the man, whose name he remembered as Hogg or Hobbs, had been introduced to him by his own brother, Fred Lehder, who knew the man as a fellow

Vietnam veteran. According to Lehder, the vice consul and an unidentified colleague offered to buy Norman's Cay from him. They planned to use the island as a Contra arms shipment base. During his testimony, Lehder also made an explosive revelation: In return for the sale, the U.S. government would give him a "green light" to bring in drugs to the United States. Lehder said he did not trust the two men, so he cut off contact with them "because I thought it could be a sting operation to capture and bring me to the United States."

Lehder also testified at Noriega's trial that he and the Medellín Cartel contributed $10 million to the U.S.-backed Nicaraguan Contra rebels in the early 1980s.

"Did the cartel give $10 million to the Contras?" Frank Rubino, Noriega's defense lawyer, asked Lehder during cross examination.

"To the best of my recollection, there was some contribution to the Contras' anti-communist movement," Lehder replied. "It could be around $10 million."

"Did you personally contribute the money?" Rubino continued.

"Apparently, I did," Lehder replied.

Lehder also acknowledged having had contact with John Hull, an American rancher based in Costa Rica at the time. For years, Contra-connected witnesses had cited Hull's ranch as a cocaine transshipment point for drugs heading to the United States and weapons to the Contras. Hull was arrested by Costa Rican authorities in January 1989 and charged with drug trafficking and violating that country's security laws. He spent two months in jail—part of it in a hospital ward because of heart problems—before friends and neighbors raised $37,500 for his bail.

Soon after, Hull fled Costa Rica, ostensibly with the help of the Reagan administration. At the time of Noriega's trial, Hull was still being sought by Costa Rica.

In 1982, the Medellín Cartel worked out a deal with Noriega in which he allowed it to use Panama as a trans-shipment point for drugs in return for a fee for the services it rendered. The following year, the cartel built a huge lab in the Darien jungle of southern Panama, about fifty miles from the Colombia border. It is believed Escobar and his associates paid as much $5 million to high-ranking Panamanian military officers and most likely Noriega, himself, to conduct their drug business and operate the lab in peace.

In 1984 the Medellín Cartel, along with the CIA, helped to finance the campaign of Noriega's candidate for President, Nicolas Barletta. Barletta was declared the winner ten days after the election, but the U.S. ambassador hid from the media information that showed Barletta had been defeated by at least four thousand votes. Political opposition parties demonstrated for weeks against the egregious fraud to no avail. Reagan welcomed the newly elected president to the Oval Office, and U.S. Secretary of State George Schultz attended Barletta's inauguration.

Noriega did arrange at least two meetings between Medellín Cartel leaders and the Colombian government in which the cartel tried to negotiate its way out of the drug trade. Noriega probably had something to do with the meeting the cartel had with former Colombian President Alphonso Lopez Michelsen, a member of one of the most prominent families in Colombia and an elder statesman in the Liberal Party.

At about the time they arrived in Panama, they learned Lopez Michelsen would be coming to Panama as one of several international dignitaries who would monitor the upcoming Panamanian elections. The Medellín Cartel leaders got word to Lopez Michelsen that they wanted to meet with him when he got to Panama. He agreed to meet and notified the Colombian government of his plans.

Jorge Ochoa recalled for PBS's "Frontline" what happened: "After Lara Bonilla, we went to Panama, and we tried to make contacts through the government... We offered the government to stop the business. No one controls the business... Pablo didn't control it, I didn't control it, or the Mexican (Rodriguez Gacha)—nobody controls the business. The control, the business, exists because of supply and demand. We offered to the government that we would stop the business. But when they say that we offered to pay the debt that was a total lie."

According to Ochoa, the cartel was anxious to make a deal because the cartel leaders wanted to live in peace with their families.

Arriving in Panama City, Panama's capital, Lopez Michelsen checked in to the same hotel at which Escobar and Jorge Ochoa were staying. Soon after, Michelsen met with the two drug lords. The three men were not strangers. It was widely believed that Lopez Michelsen had taken money from the Medellín Cartel. For instance, in 1982, Lopez Michelsen met with Medellín Cartel leaders in a hotel in Medellín, Colombia, where the drug traffickers made a contribution to his presidential campaign.

At the meeting with Lopez Michelsen, Escobar and Ochoa were polite and cordial but adamant in their denial that they had anything to do with Lara Bonilla's murder. Why were they and their families being persecuted for something they had not done, the drug kingpins complained?

Escobar and Jorge Ochoa said they represented a large group of drug traffickers in the Colombian drug trade, everybody except Lehder. They all wanted to get out of the drug trade and return to a normal and respectable life. They would stop drug trafficking in exchange for amnesty and a promise from the Colombian government that they would not be extradited to the U.S. Lopez Michelsen listened and made no promises, but said he would convey the offer to Colombian President Bentacur.

Meanwhile, the Medellín Cartel suffered a setback when the Panamanian defense forces raided the Darien lab and arrested twenty-three people. Enraged by the unexpected action, Escobar and his associates demanded that Noriega give an explanation. A meeting was arranged. Fidel Castro, who had a good relationship with Noriega, served as an intermediary to smooth things over. As a result, the twenty-three workers from the lab were released and equipment and money returned to the cartel.

The cartel had another meeting with the Colombian government to try and smooth things over, this time with Colombian Attorney General Carlos Jiminez Gomez. Jose Gonzalo Rodriguez Gacha joined Escobar and Jorge Ochoa at the meeting. It was more of the same. The cartel presented Jiminez Gomez with a six-page memorandum addressed to President Betancur in which they confirmed the assurance they had made to Lopez Michelsen at the first meeting. They had nothing to do with Lara Bonilla's murder.

Again, they promised to get out of the drug trade and return their money to Colombia, which they said would be a boon to the economy. They also promised to help with the rehabilitation of drug-addicted Colombians.

In return they wanted the government to call off its offensive, the promise of amnesty for past crimes, and the assurance that they would not be extradited to the U.S. They asked the Colombian government to inform the U.S. government of their offer. But Uncle Sam would have none of it. The U.S. Embassy leaked word of the meetings, forcing Bentacur to publicly reject the Medellín Cartel initiative.

When asked by PBS's "Frontline" why the initiative was rejected, Jorge Ochoa explained: "I'm not quite sure why they said no after we had talked two or three times with the people sent from the government. They no longer talked to us... But it would have been a great moment, and I think a lot of things would have been done, because after that a lot of violence happened. That would have been the best thing that could have happened with the government for there to be peace.

Even if he had been on good terms with his Medellín Cartel associates, Lehder would probably have not gone to Panama. Lehder simply did not trust Noriega, and he had had it with Noriega's broken promises and failure to come through on drug deals. He knew that Noriega was close to the CIA and its payroll, and he suspected that Noriega might turn all the Medellín Cartel leaders over to his sponsor if he had to save his own skin.

Later at General Noreiga's trial, Lehder tied Cuba to Nicaragua and drug trafficking when he testified that "the Cubans were in charge of the cocaine conspiracy in Nicaragua." Lehder also claimed that a top Cuban intelligence operative, with the approval of the Sandinistas, helped the Medellín Cartel organize a drug smuggling route out of Nicaragua. Lehder testified that he met twice with Raul Castro, Fidel's brother and Cuba's minster of defense, to gain permission for cocaine shipments to fly over Cuban territory on their way to Florida. "It was the Cubans who were in charge of organizing and running the cocaine smuggling network from Nicaragua to the United States," Lehder testified.

Lehder also claimed that he attended several meetings in Managua, Nicaragua's capitol, as head of Medellín Cartel's transportation operations. As a result, the Medellín Cartel was required to pay both governments of Panama and Nicaragua. Lehder never did provide specifics as to the amount paid or to whom.

No documentary evidence was presented at Noriega's trial to back up Lehder's assertions about Cuba and the Sandinistas. He could have been spinning a strong Medellín Cartel-Cuba-Nicaragua connection to gain favor with Uncle Sam so he could get a better sentencing deal.

In his trial testimony, Lehder described himself as still the head of the Medellín Cartel's transportation operations at the time. But as we have seen, reports had the cartel cutting ties with Lehder because of his bad practice of talking about cartel business in public.

Was Lehder lying to the court? Not necessarily, it is conceivable that the cartel took Lehder back into the fold because of his ability to move the cocaine to the market. Escobar and his associates were shrewd enough to recognize Lehder's value to the organization, despite his shortcomings.

Carlos Toro said this is a plausible scenario. According to Toro, Norman's Cay remained a viable transportation nexus for drug trafficking up until about 1986. "We still had the (Bahama) government in our pocket and we were moving drugs through Norman's Cay easily and effectively," Toros recalled.

Another report suggested that the cartel had made a rapprochement with Lehder while he was on the run in the jungle. He got sick with a fever, and Pablo Escobar sent a helicopter for him and brought him bring back to Medellín where he received medical attention to save his life. Even so, he was left very weak. When he recovered, Escobar hired Lehder as a bodyguard. Or at least that is the way the story went.

In July 1984, the U.S. did indict top-ranking Sandinista officials for involvement with the Medellín Cartel. The indictment was based largely on the undercover work of Barry Seale, a former Special Forces pilot in Vietnam and a TWA captain who flew cocaine shipments from Colombia to the United States for the Medellín Cartel during the 1970s and early 1980s. Carlos Toro said that, although he did not personally meet Seal, he talked to him on the phone, and that Seal had visited Norman's Cay and met with Carlos Lehder. "I believe he moved drugs for Lehder," Toro said. Seal told friends that he once made $1.5 million on a single cocaine flight to the U.S.

Ironically, in 1984, Seal was indicted on conspiracy to smuggle not cocaine but quaaludes into the country. Flipped by the DEA, Seal became an invaluable informant and managed to set up a "smoking gun" meeting that connected the Sandinistas to the Medellín Cartel.

Seal took some remarkable photos during a Nicaragua sting operation that clearly showed Pablo Escobar, Jorge Luis Ochoa Vázquez, and other members of the Medellín Cartel loading kilos of cocaine on to a C-123 transport plane. Also at the plane was Frederico Vaughan, an associate of Tomas Borges of Nicaragua's Interior Ministry, who was photographed with Sandinista soldiers helping to load the plane. According to Toro, Lehder was not at this meeting.

Seal also presented testimony before a U.S. federal grand jury that implicated Lehder as well as Escobar and Jorge Ochoa in drug trafficking. Enraged, the Medellín Cartel put a $500,000 bounty on Seal's head or $1 million if he was brought back to Colombia.

Despite the bounty, Seal refused protection. In January 1986, as part of a plea bargain agreement with the U.S. government, he began serving a six-month sentence at the Salvation Army hostel in his home town of Baton Rouge, Louisiana. At about 6 p.m. on February 19, 1986, as Seal pulled his white Cadillac Fleetwood into the parking lot of the Salvation Army, two men approached his car carrying Ingram Mac-10 guns. They killed Seal instantly.

After Seal's killing, Uncle Sam launched a federal manhunt for the Colombian hit men the Medellín Cartel sent. They were caught while trying to leave Louisiana for Colombian. In 1987, Luis Carlos Quintero-Cruz, the trigger man, and Miguel Velez and Bernardo Antonio Vasquez, accomplices, were convicted of Barry Seal's murder and sentenced to life in prison.

The official story about who killed Seal has Jorge Ochoa as being the mastermind, but Ochoa never stood trial in the U.S. for his alleged crime. Today, many believe the CIA had something to do with Seal's murder because Seal had a lot of dirt on people in the U.S government.

The killing had no impact on the Medellín Cartel. By the time of Seal's murder, Lehder and the rest of the Medellín Cartel leaders had been back in Colombia for a while. There, they were still involved with the tricky task of trying to survive while keeping their drug smuggling empires operating.

ᘓ ᘔ

CHAPTER 7

A FUGTIVE IN COLOMBIA

In the fall of 1984, Pablo Escobar, Jose Rodriguez Gacha and Fabio and Juan David Ochoa were all spotted in Medellín. Their reappearances in Colombia marked the end of the Colombian government's crackdown. Lehder also re-entered Colombia and hid among leftist guerillas in the jungle region. The Medellín Cartel brought Lehder back into the fold to serve as a go-between with the guerillas and to oversee its booming jungle operations.

Despite his fugitive status, Lehder managed to keep a high profile. His political party, the Latin Nationalist Movement (MLN), had even managed to run candidates for elections. Lehder's fleet of helicopters and private aircraft were used to distribute leaflets throughout the department of Quindio and as far away as the cities of Bogota, Medellín and Cali. The party won two out of thirteen seats in the department assembly as well a total of eleven council seats in several cities, including Armenia's capital.

Being a fugitive for almost four years was not a pleasant existence for a hard-living drug lord like Carlos Lehder. When not giving the occasional interview, the drug lord spent most of that time on farms in Colombia's rugged and pristine eastern Llanos jungle region evading capture. To keep himself occupied, he would lift weights, smoke dope, ride dirt bikes and read books with titles like *The Art of Motorcycle Maintenance* and *The Return of Eva Peron.*

Not every Medellín Cartel leader came back to Colombia. After his brief stay in Panama, Jorge Ochoa journeyed to Spain with Gilberto Rodriguez Orejuela, his boyhood friend and founding member of Colombia's Cali Cartel. At the time, the Medellín and Cali cartels were on good terms.

In Spain the two friends assumed aliases, posed as respectable businessmen and enjoyed an opulent lifestyle. However, their presence eventually attracted the attention of the Spanish authorities who launched an investigation after discovering that warrants had been issued for their arrest in the United States.

On October 17, 1985, the police arrested Ochoa and Rodriguez, and the U.S. ambassador to Spain immediately requested their extradition to the United States. Ochoa and Rodriguez Orejuela were extradited to Colombia instead, where a judge quickly acquitted Rodriguez Orejuela of cocaine trafficking charges. Ochoa faced similar charges in Medellín, but he stood trial in Cartagena, not for drug trafficking but for smuggling 125 bulls into Colombia. Ochoa was found guilty and sentenced to two years in jail. Associates on Ochoa's behalf reportedly paid about $660,000 to "persuade" the judge to give Ochoa bail. The judge conveniently overlooked the more serious charge Ochoa faced in Medellín and ordered him to report to the court every two weeks.

Ochoa did not stick around. Once out on bail, he opted to flee Cartagena and become a fugitive. In his book, *Whitewash,* Simon Strong explained what happened: "The government launched a nationwide hunt for Ochoa, but to no avail: the joke in Medellín was that the police had searched every building except the one Ochoa was in."

Carlos Lehder is believed to have fled to Spain for a time after the Colombian government crackdown, but, while there, he did not associate with Ochoa and Rodriguez, which helps to explain why Lehder was never picked up by Spanish police surveillance. After the arrest of Ochoa and Rodriguez Orejuela, Lehder fled across the border to Portugal.

From Portugal, Lehder went to Cuba where he was asked to leave after two weeks, ostensibly because of his bad behavior. Lehder spent some time in Mexico where he made some controversial public comments before returning to Colombia in early 1985.

Despite the danger, Lehder still could not keep his mouth shut. He gave an interview to a Cali newspaper, vowing to become a "revolutionary hero" and declaring his intention to join a faction of the revolutionary group, M-19.

In February 1985, Crazy Charlie gave his famous speech in the Colombian jungle to Spanish television while he sat in a chair with his back to the river. The bearded and shaggy-haired fugitive praised Hitler ("until someone surpasses him, he shall be the greatest warrior the world has ever seen"), denounced "American imperialism" and the U.S.-Colombia extradition treaty, denied the holocaust, dismissed claims he had anything to do with Lara Bonilla's killing, and played to Colombian national sentiment by ranting about forming a five-hundred-thousand-man army to defend Colombia's sovereignty.

During the interview, Lehder never did reveal what he did for a living. Colombians watched in awe and wondered how the most wanted man in Colombia could operate so brazenly in the open. Lehder and the other powerful Colombian drug lords were showing themselves to be untouchable.

Lehder's remarkable interview with Spanish television embarrassed the DEA, which claimed it had been looking for Lehder high and low, yet somehow a Spanish TV station had managed to find him. The interview pressured the DEA to step up its hunt for the U.S.'s number one most wanted Colombian drug dealer. The DEA questioned the Spanish correspondent who had interviewed Crazy Charlie, but he told the agency nothing. All the DEA could gather from its investigation was that Lehder was believed to be hiding at a place east of Bogota called *Hacienda Abundancia* (Ranch of the Abundance).

The CIA viewed the tape of the interview at its Imaging Section, Central Headquarters, Langley, Virginia. Technicians were able to determine the approximate time of the interview and the general area where the interview took place. A National Security Agency (NSA) satellite used to get a better look at the area identified a stucco house the U.S. authorities believed could be Lehder's.

In the morning hours of August 8, 1985, a team of heavily-armed Colombian federal police and DEA agents made their way through the jungle and surrounded the house. Automatic gunfire came from inside the house until shooters inside the house surrendered. The authorities confiscated twelve pounds of cocaine and nearly $2 million in cash, but they found no Carlos Lehder.

Portraits of Adolph Hitler and Eva Braun, his mistress, covered the walls of the hacienda. The raiding party had little doubt that this was Lehder's hideout. In what had become a familiar story, the authorities had again failed to capture Lehder. In April of 1985, for instance, Crazy Charlie had narrowly escaped capture at a cattle ranch in Meta province. The authorities captured nine of Lehder's bodyguards and confiscated 350 kilos cocaine and $1.6 million in cash. On another raid, Lehder had to scurry into the bush, carrying a machine gun and wearing nothing but his underpants. The authorities found more cash—$1,678,680 in cardboard liquor boxes.

Despite the government crackdown, the Medellín Cartel continued to grow in wealth and power, and by early 1985, it was no doubt the world's most powerful drug trafficking organization. While U.S. law enforcement claimed more seizures in 1985 than before, the price of cocaine kept dropping, and that, said economists, was a sure indicator more cocaine was on the American streets than ever before. In one fifteen-day period in January 1985, authorities had seized more cocaine (2,250 kilos) than they had seized the entire year of 1981

In recognition of their criminal success, Lehder appeared in a *Newsweek* magazine cover story along with associates Escobar and Jorge Ochoa. Titled, "Colombia's Kings of Cocaine," the cover story concluded that "Together they have become Colombia's cocaine overlords—a small tight-knit clique of smugglers almost as rich as the Colombian government itself."

Given its power, the Medellín Cartel continued its narcoterrorism campaign in Colombia, using so-called *sicarios*, mostly teenage killers recruited from the slum sections of Colombia's Medellín City, to do their dirty work. The *sicarios* cared little for their personal safety, for, as Simon Strong writes in his book, *Whitewash*: "The adolescent contract killers preferred to live one minute as somebody than thirty years as nobody."

The *sicarios* liked to ride through clogged streets and pull up alongside a target's car and empty their guns at their victims and their victims' bodyguards. *Sicarios* loved their mothers and consumer goods and were religiously superstitious. As one 16-year-old *sicario* said in an interview: "I am going to die, but my mother will remember me because I got her a beautiful new refrigerator."

The people the *sicarios* murdered included a long list of police officers, journalists, government officials, and presidential candidates. They even took on Colombia's Supreme Court. On November 6, 1985, approximately thirty-five M-19 guerrillas working for the Medellín Cartel stormed the Colombia Palace of Justice in Bogota. Within minutes, the guerrillas had 250 hostages, including Alfonso Reyes Echandia, the Chief Justice of Colombia's Supreme Court, and many of the twenty-four Supreme Court justices. For the next twenty-four hours, thousands of soldiers and police tried retaking the building, but the more heavily armed and well-entrenched guerillas fought them off. When the government finally prevailed, twenty hostages lay dead, including Chief Justice Reyes.

It is widely believed the Medellín Cartel paid the guerrillas to take the Supreme Court building and destroy the extradition records they found there because they contained incriminating evidence against the cartel. Many of the justices favored upholding the extradition treaty with the United States and were scheduled to vote on the issue in the near future.

The bold attack set the tenor for the next decade in Colombia. By 1990, the Medellín Cartel had murdered more than two hundred court officials and at least forty Colombian judges.

Despite the intimidation and narcoterrorism, President Virgilio Barco implemented the Colombian-United States Extradition Treaty in 1986 after he took office. The Medellín Cartel responded by ratcheting up its ruthless terrorist campaign against the state. Calling themselves the Extraditables, the cartel vowed, "better a grave in Colombia than a jail cell in the United States," and began to target prominent supporters of extradition, as well as get-tough-on-drugs officials.

The Medellín Cartel wanted to assassinate one particular Colombian official who had become a major obstacle to its best-laid plans: Colonel Jaime Ramirez Gomez, head of the National Police. He was credited with launching the country's first real initiative against the country's powerful drug traffickers: the take-down of the big Medellín Cartel lab at Tranqui-

capture. Then Uncle Sam made an aggressive move for regime change. In December, 1989, the U.S. sent in 25,000 troops to overthrow Noriega in what became known as Operation Just Cause.

It was a remarkably short operation, although it became controversial because hundreds of Panamanians lost their lives, and Panama City and El Chorillo experienced extensive damage during the operation. For twenty-two days, Noriega managed to elude the U.S. military before desperately seeking asylum in the Vatican Embassy before finally surrendering to the DEA on January 3, 1990. The next day he was brought to Miami where he awaited trial on drug trafficking charges.

General Noriega faced the possibility of decades in jail, but Uncle Sam first needed solid evidence to convict him. That is where Carlos Lehder saw his opportunity to perhaps one day get out of jail. Whether Lehder sought out the government in return for a deal or whether it was Uncle Sam who approached Crazy Charlie and convinced him to testify is unclear. But a week before Noriega's trial, Lehder also agreed to give testimony in return for a reduction of his sentence of life plus 135 years without parole. A deal was remarkable in that Lehder acknowledged he had never met Noriega, and critics claimed his testimony was not necessary to convict Noriega.

Since his extradition from Colombia, Lehder had always contended that the U.S. government had kid-

landia in Colombia's jungle region. The bust had infuriated the cartel, and it was itching for the opportunity for revenge.

At the time, Ramirez Gomez, no doubt, was the star member of Colombian law enforcement. "At the beginning of 1986, he was undeniably the most famous narc in the world—a legend in his own country, revered by the DEA, sought for his counsel by the police from Lima to Washington," write Guy Gugliotta and Jeff Leen in *Kings of Cocaine.*

Although highly respected by the U.S. Drug Enforcement Administration and the U.S. Embassy in Bogota, Ramirez Gomez received little support from the Colombian government. He could have easily played the corruption game, but when the Medellín Cartel tried to bribe him, he refused, remaining steadfast even when the cartel threatened to kill him and he began receive about ten death threats a week. Ramirez Gomez was officially relieved of his post as head of the National Police's Anti-Narcotics Unit on December 31, 1985, and after forty days he quietly returned to active duty with the National Police.

In his three-year tenure as head of the Unit, he was credited with seizing twenty-seven tons of cocaine; arresting 7, 941 men and 1,405 women; and confiscating 2,783 trucks, 1060 cars, 83 boats and 116 planes.

But the Medellín Cartel was relentless and put a contract on Ramirez Gomez's life. On November 17, 1986, assassins caught up with their target and machine gunned the colonel to death in front of his wife. Remarkably, the Colombian Defense Ministry denied a move to honor Colonel Ramirez posthumously for his anti-narcotics work.

Colonel Jaime Ramirez Gomez had gone down in the war on drugs. That was the price one paid for being honest and brave. As a military man, he had bodyguards, but Guillermo Cano Izaza, editor-in-chief for *El Espectador*, Colombia's second largest newspaper, had no such protection. Still, he wrote frequently about drugs in his editorial page column "*Libreta de Apuntes*" ("Notebook") and called for tougher laws against the country's drug traffickers. He was disturbed that several prominent Colombians opposed extradition of criminals to the United States and wanted to legalize drugs as a way to avoid narcotics-related violence.

On December 17, 1986, a *sicario* traveling on a motorcycle in busy downtown Bogota traffic gunned down Cano Izaza. The brazen killing of a member of the Fourth Estate shocked even cynical Colombians. The authorities investigated, and in early 1988 announced that they had solved Cano Izaza's murder. It was a contract killing carried out by a Medellín Cartel assassination squad known as *Los Priscos*.

As brazen as the killings of Ramirez Gomez, Cano Izaza and the Supreme Court justices were, Lehder and his associates topped themselves for audacity when they went after Enrique Parejo Gonzalez, Rodrigo Lara Bonilla's replacement as Colombia's justice minister.

When Parejo Gonzalez received word that the cartel was going to try to assassinate him, the Colombian government sent him to Hungary where it was thought he would be safe behind the Iron Curtain. But as boxer Joe Louis once said about an opponent: "He can run but he can't hide." In January 1987, assassins caught up with Parejo Gonzalez in a blizzard on a Budapest street and shot him five times. Parejo Gonzalez survived the attack, thanks to the surgical skill of Hungarian doctors who performed two operations to remove the bullets. In 1994, he returned to Colombia where he ran unsuccessfully for president.

During his nearly four years on the run, many rumors abounded about Lehder's whereabouts. Then at the end of 1986, the authorities got a break when Colombian police received intelligence information that Lehder was in the Medellín area where he planned to start a cocaine manufacturing operation and meet with Escobar.

The intelligence then got more specific. The authorities were told that they should stake out a farm about twenty miles outside Medellín near the small town of Rionegro. How the authorities got that information remains open to speculation. In one report, a man walked into the office of a high-ranking police officer in Medellín in January 1987 and asked how much the authorities were willing to pay for information about the whereabouts of one of the Medellín Cartel leaders. The police told the man that they had no money for that kind of information.

The would-be informant told the police to think about it and he would call back in a few days. When the man called again, the police told him that the U.S. Embassy was willing to pay $50,000 for reliable information. The informant told the police where the drug lord was hiding, but did not give his name.

Another report has a *campesino* watching the farm and noticing a "bunch of men" shouting, playing music, and literally "raising hell" for a couple of days. On February 3, 1987, at daybreak, a twenty-man elite police force moved in on the farm. A gunfight broke out, and half an hour later, the fifteen men inside were arrested. They were all in their underwear. Only when the police looked at the suspects' papers did they know the names of the men they had captured. In a weird twist, Lehder and his men posed for photos.

Some reports had the Colombian police crashing what was a homosexual orgy. A police captain and a member of the raiding party told the *Sunday Times* of London: "The lookout was too hung over to see us. A few feet away he looked up, yelled and fired a machine gun. But I knocked him down with a bullet in the hip. A few more rounds and a man came out with his hands in the air saying, 'Don't shoot, I'm Carlos Lehder.'"

Police Major William Lemus, who headed the operation, could hardly contain himself. Pointing to the suspect dressed in a T-shirt and blue jeans, he shouted excitedly, "We've caught him! This is Carlos Lehder!"

Lehder reportedly muttered: "This is the one place I never expected you'd catch me."

Back at the Rionegro police station, the phone began to ring off the hook. The general message: "Lemus, who do you think you are? You are dead!"

The police immediately informed government officials of the good news. The minister of justice assured the president that Lehder could be extradited immediately.

Meanwhile, Lehder was taken to police headquarters in Bogota and then hustled to the airport where a DEA turboprop was waiting to whisk him away to the U.S. At the airport, Lehder nearly collapsed when he finally realized what was happening. On the flight, however, he regained his arrogant aplomb. When offered a cigarette, he reportedly replied, "No thank you, I only smoke marijuana."

Within ten days of Lehder's capture, the DEA had Lemus and his family on a plane and out of the country. Remarkably, despite a few initial threats for revenge, the Medellín Cartel did not retaliate. This has led to speculation that Pablo Escobar may have set up Lehder for arrest. After all, many reports had indicated that Escobar was embarrassed and fed up with Lehder's crazy antics.

How out control had Lehder become? At one of the cartel parties, Lehder reportedly tried to seduce one of Escobar's favorite bodyguards, but was rebuffed. Feeling insulted, Lehder was said to have shot and killed the man, who happened to be one of Escobar's favorite bodyguards.

Whether this incident happened or whether it had anything to do with Lehder's capture is really immaterial. The U.S. government now had its biggest prize in its war on drugs. Incredibly, it had taken less than eighteen hours from Lehder's arrest to have him on a plane to the U.S.

ᴥ

CHAPTER 8

THE TRIAL

Carlos Lehder was the biggest drug kingpin ever extradited to the U.S., which made his trial the most publicized and high profile in the country's history. It would last eight months, cost taxpayers several million dollars and include more than one hundred witnesses taking the stand for Uncle Sam.

Several individuals did not testify; however, they did provide valuable information that helped build the case against Lehder. One of them was Carlos Toro, Lehder's boyhood friend and associate, who was now on the outs with Crazy Charlie. Toro had been in an altercation with one of Lehder's associates after Toro had accused the associate of stealing money from Lehder and the Medellín Cartel. After threatening to go to Lehder and the cartel bosses with the allegation, the altercation ended with Toro having to shoot the associate in self-defense.

The associate survived, but Toro was in trouble with the Medellín Cartel. Toro called Lehder to explain what had happened. He expected his boss to understand; instead, Lehder told him, "You shot one of my men? You're dead."

Toro said he was then set up for a murder that he believed Medellín Cartel hitmen committed. Interrogated by law enforcement, Toro was cleared of the murder, but he let slip that he had bought fuel for planes owned by the Medellín Cartel. Now the authorities could nail Toro for conspiracy to traffic cocaine. He faced a mandatory fifteen-year sentence if convicted. Toro did not like his chances in court, so he worked out a deal with the DEA in which he would be an informant for ninety days in return for pleading no contest to the conspiracy charge.

The deal meant that he would remain free and his criminal record, sealed. Toro proved invaluable in providing information about cartel assets, including banks, stash houses, residences and other properties.

Well aware of the Medellín Cartel's reputation for extreme violence, American authorities continued to expect some kind of retaliation as revenge for their legal coup. One U.S. department source confided to the *Toronto Star* newspaper: "We are going crazy trying to figure out how to deal with security."

Soon after Lehder's arrival in the U.S., wild rumors circulated, which heightened the tension surrounding the trial. One report had a thirty-five-hundred-strong army being smuggled into the U.S. to rescue Lehder, while another report speculated that Colombian guerrillas planned to show up in the U.S. to destroy a sports arena during a sporting event.

As the trial began, Lehder's demeanor did not exactly inspire confidence on the part of U.S. officials that they had the trial under control. One U.S. newspaper wrote, as the case moved to trial, "Lehder sits (in the courtroom), smiling frequently as if he knows something."

So dangerous did Uncle Sam view Lehder that the authorities had him sent to the federal maximum-security prison at Marion, Illinois, which at the time Uncle Sam used to house its most dangerous prisoners. He was one of the few pre-trial detainees in Marion's history. When Lehder's lawyers complained about the distance they had to travel to meet with their client, Lehder was moved to the federal prison in Talladega, Alabama, before finally being transferred to the federal prison in Atlanta.

Despite being kept in total isolation and away from the prison population, Lehder was constantly plagued by the incessant noise in the unruly prisons. Lehder's lawyers complained that at the federal prison in Atlanta, primal screams from a section of the prison housing 1,800 prisoners from the Mariel boatlift "punctuate the air minute by minute."

Security for the trial was unprecedented. Each day, Lehder arrived at the court via military helicopter under heavy guard. The police placed sharpshooters strategically around the courthouse when the trial began. The metal detectors were so sensitive that many spectators in the courtroom had to remove their shoes because the nails in them set off an alarm. The authorities, moreover, hooded the parking meters to prevent parking within four blocks of the Jacksonville courthouse. In a day long before the 9-11 mega event happened, everyone entering the courtroom was searched and screened.

The court appointed a lawyer to handle Lehder's case, but facing decades in prison if convicted, Lehder went shopping for the best legal counsel money could buy. Interestingly, several top-notch lawyers turned Lehder down, not because they had any qualms defending him, but because they feared getting entangled in a new money laundering law that made it a felony for a lawyer to accept a fee if it came from illegal sources.

The trial featured a face-off between lawyers with contrasting styles. Defending Lehder were two well-known and respected criminal defense lawyers from Miami: Ed Shohat and Jose Quinon. Shohat had extensive experience handling Colombian drug cases, as well as a reputation for honesty and competence.

Given his aggressive style in the courtroom, Shohat handled most of the defense arguments in court. Quinon, a Cuban American, was a former state prosecutor known for his ability to charm juries and courtroom personnel.

Shohat's and Quinon's counsel did not come cheap. It was reported that Lehder may have paid his lawyers $2.5 million in legal fees.

Heading the prosecution was Robert Merkle, a prosecutor whose tenacious courtroom style had earned him the nickname of "Mad Dog." Born in Washington, D.C., and raised mostly in Greenville, S.C., Merkle earned undergraduate and law degrees from the University of Notre Dame before moving to Florida in 1977 to work in a state attorney's office. He joined the U.S. Attorney's office in 1981 and was appointed head of the office the following year. During his flamboyant run as prosecutor, he obtained indictments against three sitting Florida representatives, two judges, three prosecutors, and dozens of bankers, attorneys and postal workers. Critics acknowledged Merkle's legal skills but questioned his methods. Defense attorneys decried what they viewed as abusive, bullying tactics in the courtroom. They compared them to McCarthyism and called for U.S. Justice Department investigations. Florida Governor Bob Martinez once tried to get Merkle fired for calling Martinez a liar. Meanwhile, newspapers campaigned for the prosecutor's ouster. Yet, despite the controversy, Merkle was always cleared of any inappropriate behavior.

"Bob was one of those rare individuals who was truly larger than life," John Fitzgibbons, who worked under Merkle in the U.S. attorney's office for four years, told the *St. Petersburg Times* in 2003. "In the courtroom, he was as good a trial lawyer as there was in America. As a boss, he was probably the most complex, difficult and demanding boss you could imagine."

At the preliminary hearing, Lehder's legal counsel, at that time court-appointed, claimed that Pablo Escobar had set her client up. A few days later, a letter from Escobar arrived at the offices of *El Tiempo*, Colombia's leading newspaper. The drug lord conceded that he had "personal quarrels" with Lehder, but it was beneath him to do such a "low and cowardly act" as to betray him to the authorities.

As the U.S. government prepared for trial, the IRS took a big shot at Lehder by filing a $300 million lien against the drug lord. The IRS estimated that Lehder had earned $300 million smuggling cocaine in 1979 and 1980. Later, in May 1988, soon after Lehder's conviction, the U.S authorities took another crack at Lehder when it tried to seize Lehder's property in the Bahamas. The jury in the Lehder trial had determined that it was legal to do so.

But the Bahamian authorities decided differently, warning Uncle Sam that any move by U.S officials to seize Lehder's property would be blocked. The Bahamian government planned to seize the property for itself since Bahamian law allowed them to confiscate the property of those convicted of drug trafficking outside the Bahamas. The Bahamian government had approved a treaty with the U.S. under which the Bahamas would have allowed the U.S. to confiscate property of foreigners convicted abroad, but the U.S. had failed to pass similar legislation. Lehder owned millions of dollars' worth of property in the Bahamas, including a condominium, two houses, an airstrip, hotel, marina, six companies, and about half of Norman's Cay.

Since the trial was one of the biggest in U.S. history, delays were inevitable, and the trial date was pushed back from the spring to the early fall. To keep the trial moving, District Judge Howard W. Melton sternly and firmly refused to grant many of the delays requested by the defense.

Lehder's lawyers publicly questioned whether their client could get a fair trial, complaining that the news media had made Lehder such a well-known and notorious public figure that newspaper headlines used Lehder's last name without having to further identify who he was.

Lehder's lawyers filed a motion for change of venue, arguing that the prosecution was attempting to try Lehder in the newspapers. By violating Lehder's sixth amendment rights, the lawyers argued, he was being denied the right to a fair and speedy trial by an impartial jury.

Judge Melton denied the motion, thus refusing to recognize the harmful effects that adverse publicity would have on Lehder's defense and his ability to obtain a fair trial by an impartial jury. Shohat and Quinones continued to file motions.

The basis of the case against Lehder was an eleven-count indictment filed on September 18, 1981, against him, Jack Reed, Lehder’s pilot who had many drug runs to the U.S. for Lehder, and two other co-defendants. Count one charged Lehder and Reed with engaging in a conspiracy to import cocaine from June 1978 to September 1980 in violation of U.S. law. Counts two through eleven charged Lehder with nine acts of importing and possessing cocaine with intent to distribute and engaging in a continuing criminal enterprise.

Jack Carlton Reed left Norman’s Cay in 1983 and had all but disappeared off the DEA’s radar screen. Then, in September 1986, the DEA received an anonymous letter disclosing that Reed was living in a small bungalow near the remote village of Portobelo on the Isthmus of Panama.

Reed had long since left the drug trade and he was content to live a simple existence away from civilization. In his memoir *Buccaneer,* written with MayCay Beeler, Reed described his Panamanian experience as a virtual paradise and the most rewarding chapter of his life.

"I adopted a spartan Robinson Crusoe-type lifestyle," Reed wrote. "It is here, in a primitive Panamanian paradise, in an anti-establishment, remote home-steading environment that I finally found the high quality of life I sought my entire life."

For Reed it became a paradise interrupted when the DEA began staking out the place. After receiving information that Lehder planned to set up a cocaine laboratory in the area, the agency figured that sooner or later Lehder would show up.

Sure enough, one of Lehder's old associates was seen visiting the bungalow in the company of several other drug traffickers. Then the DEA learned that the Colombian authorities had arrested Lehder. The agency decided now was the time to arrest Reed before he discovered that Lehder had been arrested, and he tried to flee.

At 5 a.m. on February 6, 1987, two teams of Panamanian commandos, accompanied by DEA agents, cut through heavy jungle and reached Reed's bungalow where they surrounded it.

They quickly cut off any escape by sea. When they called for Reed to surrender, a tall thin figure burst out of the bungalow and headed for the jungle. Reed surrendered when he saw the assault rifles turned on him.

Reed claimed to be a simple farmer named John Williams, but he didn't fool his pursuers and was arrested. In his memoir, Reed called his arrest a kidnapping. "I can think of no other word to describe how I felt for a very long time."

Just days after Lehder's capture, Reed was on his way to Jacksonville, Florida, where he was arraigned and held without bond under tight security in a separate location from Lehder.

By the time Lehder's trial began on November 17, 1988, Bob Merkle and his prosecution team was ready for legal war. As one news report described the situation, "...for Lehder the trial was a nightmarish version of "This is Your Life." The prosecution had a solid case based on a huge and impressive body of evidence documenting Lehder's criminal career from his early days at Danbury to the mid-1980s.

Merkle's objective in court was to make Lehder a bigger-than-life drug lord, so he tried to blame him for being the criminal largely responsible for America's cocaine plague. To make his point, Merkle came up with a brilliant analogy, dubbing Crazy Charlie "The Henry Ford of Cocaine."

The lead witness for the prosecution would be Lehder's former partner, George Jung. Lehder and Jung had gone their separate ways in the late 1970s after Lehder cut him out of the drug smuggling pipeline that had made millions in profits for them.

After the split, Jung continued to operate as a successful drug dealer and make millions. He eventually got married to a Colombian woman and they had a daughter together. In 1987, when the daughter was only one year old, Jung was arrested at his mansion on Nauset Beach, near Eastham, Massachusetts. Sentenced to ten years in prison, Jung skipped bail and fled the country. When Jung got involved in another drug deal in Florida, he was betrayed by a long-time friend secretly working for the DEA, and arrested.

George Jung described to PBS's "Frontline" what happened: "We were facing ten years mandatory sentences in Massachusetts and so I thought it best to leave. I was on the run from Massachusetts and I was looking for a pilot to fly another load and my intentions were to go down to Colombia and live. I ran into a pilot friend of mine, who used to fly pot for me in the '60s, and unbeknownst to me he was working for the DEA...and he wined and dined me... and I sold the load down in Colombia and it was all sponsored by the DEA... and when the load came in I was busted and that was the end of it all."

Jung had always felt betrayed by his former friend, and he wanted to get even. The federal authorities had approached Jung in 1986 while he was prison with a proposal that he travel to Colombia in an attempt to lure Lehder into a trap. Whether Jung would have agreed to the plan is unclear, but before the plan could be implemented, Lehder was captured.

Jung had said he had no intention of testifying against Lehder, but then he learned Lehder had sent a letter to President George Bush offering to cooperate. The story made headlines in the *Miami Herald.* Lehder's attorneys denied their client wanted to turn informant, but his old associate Jung read the story and was livid.

So Lehder wanted to snitch? Jung knew quite a lot himself about Lehder and his drug trafficking activities. Jung sat down and wrote a letter detailing what he knew about his former boss and the Colombian drug trade. Jung called the authorities and told them that he would go to Jacksonville, Florida, to testify. Jung made a phone call and was taken to Jacksonville to be interviewed. After vetting Jung's story, Uncle Sam decided Jung would be a witness—the very first witness in Lehder's trial.

Vesco is not named in the Lehder indictment but Jung mentioned him at trial as having a business interest in Norman's Cay. Jung also testified that Lehder had said Vesco introduced him to Fidel Castro.

Kehm, the former manager of a company that owned land on Norman's Cay, testified to being threatened several times with death by Lehder and Jack Carlton Reed, a co-defendant, when he refused to leave the island. Eventually, however, Kehm did leave.

Kehm testified that on a trip back to the island to retrieve his furniture "we went to the main dock and I ran into Robert Vesco, of all people." After he told Vesco about problems in retrieving his personal property, Kehm said, "He (Vesco) told me the best advice he could give me was to get off the island and keep my nose out of other people's business."

In December 1987, United States Attorney Merkle identified Vesco as a co-conspirator in Lehder's trial. In arguing that the testimony of Charles Kehm about his conversation with Vesco was admissible as evidence, Merkle said the details were a "co-conspirator's testimony."

After Jung testified, a fascinating range of witnesses took the stand. Andrew Barnes, a 32-year-old British pilot, testified, "I made millions of dollars but blew almost everything crashing planes, getting out of jail, bribing officials." In return for his testimony, government prosecutors gave Barnes immunity on a wide range of charges and promised him a maximum term of seven years.

Steve Yakovac, who had befriended Lehder in a Colombian prison and later worked for Lehder, talked about lugging a scuba equipment bag with a deposit of $994,765 to the Bank of Nova Scotia in Nassau. The money weighed 120 pounds, and the bank charged one percent of the total, or about $110,000, to count the money.

Lehder loved Canada, testified former wife Yemel Nacel. To meet clients in Montreal and Toronto, Lehder would fly from Colombia and Panama. Yemel also told the court that Lehder had dated the daughter of Robert Vesco when Vesco lived in the Bahamas.

Eben Mann, a Continental Airlines pilot admitted making three cocaine-smuggling flights for Lehder for which he was paid $75,000, but he acknowledged to lying earlier on the witness stand. Mann said he was granted immunity from prosecution and advised of perjury recantation laws, which protect those who immediately correct false testimony. Mann also said he lied when he denied that he and Lehder had discussed falsely registering aircraft.

In other testimony, Russ O'Hara, a Palm Springs, California, disk jockey, who also received immunity for his testimony, showed home movies of Norman's Cay and testified about drug flights he made for Lehder. O'Hara said he began working for Lehder in 1978 as a co-pilot.

Lehder was convicted on May 21, 1988, of all eleven counts of the indictment against him. As the sentencing took place on July 20, 1988, Judge Melton allowed Lehder to address the court. Sporting a full beard and speaking perfect English, Lehder ranted for nearly half an hour against the evidence presented in court, claiming he was a political prisoner who had been kidnapped. Further, Lehder claimed, he was really against drug abuse.

Judge Melton was not impressed. He told the convicted drug lord that the sentence he was about hand down was going to send a message to anyone involved in drug trafficking. Then the Judge lowered the hammer, sentencing Lehder to the maximum-life without parole, plus 135 years. Co-defendant Jack Carlton Reed's sentence was also harsh: two consecutive life terms and a fine of $2 million. It was a good bet that both men would be spending the rest of their lives behind bars.

☙ ❧

CHAPTER 9

CRAZY CHARLIE – THE LEGEND

With Lehder's conviction, the U.S. government claimed a big victory in its war on drugs, boasting to the media that they had brought down the "Henry Ford" of cocaine transportation, a man whose criminal genius had made possible the cocaine epidemic that was plaguing the U.S. Privately, federal authorities acknowledged that Lehder's conviction would not make even a brief dip in the still-growing tide of cocaine into the US.

The drug trade had changed. While it was still drug business as usual, the transportation system that Lehder has established was no longer the major hub for illegal drug distribution. The South Florida Drug Task Force had such a successful crackdown on drug traffickers that the bad guys had switched from the Caribbean to Mexico as the route to move cocaine across the 2,000-mile U.S.-Mexican border. By the mid-1980s, the border had become the major smuggling route for cocaine into the U.S.

There had been fears that the Medellín Cartel would retaliate in some way as a warning to Uncle Sam not to come after them. There was some evidence that this could happen. In February 1987, soon after Lehder's extradition, U.S. Ambassador Charles Gillespie left Bogota for the United States after his staff received intelligence that cocaine cartel members planned to kidnap and exchange him for Lehder. Gillespie had been on the ABC-TV program "Nightline" via satellite prior to his departure from Bogota and had expressed considerable concern for his safety. But his departure was so sudden that the day it happened Gillespie's own staff at the U.S. Embassy in Bogota was not notified.

Lehder had brazenly continued to arrange cocaine transactions from his Florida jail cell while awaiting trial. This revelation came out after Lehder's ex-wife, Yemel Nacel, made a plea agreement with the U.S. government. Nacel was one of nine people who entered guilty pleas in the so-called "Son of Lehder" case. Nacel told the court that she was pleading guilty to a charge of conspiracy to distribute five kilograms or more of cocaine. She faced a maximum fifteen-year prison term and a $4 million fine.

Others pleading guilty in the case included John Lee Moeller, who faced twenty years in prison and forfeiture of about $2 million in property, including land in

Tequesta, Florida, $896,000 cash from a safe deposit box, and proceeds of $473,000 owed to him on loans, and Richard James Barile, who was accused of being instrumental in trafficking cocaine for Lehder in the 1970s and who now faced eight years under a plea agreement.

Even before Lehder went to trial and was convicted, Uncle Sam had its eye on the next big fish in the war on drugs. He was none other than Panama's General Manuel Noriega, ironically, the long-time U.S. ally who had been on the CIA's payroll since as early as 1967. From the 1960s until the 1980s, Noriega reportedly received upwards of $100,000 per year from the CIA before increasing his salary to $200,000 per year.

According to Noam Chomsky, noted critic of U.S. foreign policy, the U.S. government knew Noriega was involved in drug trafficking since at least 1972 when the Nixon administration considered assassinating him. In 1983, a U.S. Senate committee concluded that "Panama was a major center for the laundering of drug funds and drug trafficking." Still, the U.S. government considered Noriega a "valuable asset" and continued to protect him. And despite the growing evidence to the contrary, Noriega stayed on the CIA payroll.

Gradually, however, Noriega began to fall out of favor with his American benefactors, especially after the growing charges of corruption could not be ignored. Most disturbingly, Noriega was linked to the Latin American drug trade, and it became increasingly difficult for the U.S. government to ignore the reality that Noriega was a valuable asset to the Medellín Cartel.

We have seen how Noriega has provided "services" to the cartel by laundering their money and allowing them to find refuge in Panama when the heat was on in Colombia. General Noriega also cut a deal with Escobar and the Medellín Cartel in 1982, which allowed drug kingpins to ship cocaine through Panama for $100,000 per load. The two had met the previous year when Noriega mediated negotiations for the release of kidnap victim Marta Ochoa, the sister of the Ochoa drug kingpins.

In 1987, a former officer of the Panamanian defense force publicly accused Noriega of cooperating with Colombian drug producers. The following year, two U.S. federal grand juries in Florida indicted Noriega on charges of drug trafficking and racketeering and the CIA took him off its payroll. Then opposition candidates in the presidential election were stopped and beaten up by Noriega's thugs, giving more ammunition to those U.S. decision makers who wanted to see him go.

A series of incidents that culminated in the death of an American soldier compelled President George Bush to impose strict sanctions on Panama and offer a $1 million reward for information leading to his

napped him, given that there was no extradition treaty in place between the two countries. During his testimony in the Noriega trial, Lehder described how Colombian police captured him and brought him to Bogota where hooded military men and U.S officials took him into custody.

"I was handcuffed and placed in the toilet of the aircraft and tied up in the toilet," Lehder testified. He said he was flown first to the U.S. base in Guantanamo Bay, Cuba, and then to Tampa, Florida. As part of his agreement to testify, Lehder dropped his $92 million lawsuit against former U.S. Attorney General Edwin Meese and former DEA administrator Francis Mullen.

During his own trial in 1988, Lehder had been portrayed as the monster that had been largely responsible for the drug epidemic in America. At Noriega's trial in 1992, Crazy Charlie was turned into a respectable government witness whom the U.S. government said had the goods on the general.

At his own trial, Lehder was considered so dangerous a defendant that he sat shackled for the trial's duration. But during Noriega's trial in Miami, he wore no shackles and was dressed smartly in a tie and suit. During one recess he could be seen shaking hands with a member of the prosecution team.

Prosecutor Robert Merkle, who had thought he had put Lehder behind bars for good, was outraged by the deal Lehder brokered to testify against Noriega in 1988. "First of all, Lehder's testimony was entirely gratuitous and unnecessary for a conviction of Noriega," Merkle told one reporter. "Second, they gave a deal to the guy (Lehder) who was directing the bad activities to convict someone who was following directions (Noriega)." Meanwhile, many observers wondered if Lehder had conned Uncle Sam and would someday be free.

In his Noriega trial testimony, Lehder told the court about Noriega's links to the Medellín Cartel, claiming that the general had been mainly responsible for shipping cocaine from Colombia through Panama to the U.S. from 1982 to 1984. Interestingly, not one other government witness at the Noriega trial mentioned Lehder as having any role in Panama.

A lot of his testimony was explosive and made for juicy newspaper headlines. Lehder claimed that the Medellín Cartel had given money to both the Sandinistas and the Contras, but he was blocked by the court from answering questions about an unpublished interview in which he thought the contributions would give him a "green light" for shipping cocaine to the U.S. He was also prevented from testifying about allegations that he had received a letter in the early 1980s from an aide to then Vice President George Bush. The contents of the letter were not released.

Lehder said that Fidel Castro mediated a 1984 dispute between Noriega and the Medellín Cartel that probably saved the dictator from assassination. One federal official in the courtroom told the press: "I never thought I'd see anything like this. If you followed drug trafficking, it is truly historic. It takes my breath away."

The fate of General Manuel Noriega in the Miami courtroom was never in doubt. On September 16, 1992, Noriega was convicted and sentenced to forty years in prison on eight counts of drug trafficking, racketeering and money laundering. His sentence was later reduced to thirty years. When U.S. authorities released him in 2007, he would face extradition requests from France and Panama.

Quickly, Noriega's lawyers sought a new trial for the deposed Panama dictator. Attorneys Frank Rubino and Jon May argued that federal prosecutors made a series of secret deals to induce incriminating testimony from prospective witnesses at Noriega's trial. Lehder was called to testify again at a hearing by attorneys for Noriega. Lehder said he stood by his testimony at the trial as being "the truth and nothing but the truth."

Lehder, however, soon changed his mind. In the fall of 1995, he wrote a letter of complaint to a Miami district judge, claiming that the prosecutors duped him into testifying against the general in 1991 and asking permission to recant his testimony. Lehder claimed that the U.S. government had reneged on a deal to cut his own sentence to thirty years, which would have made him eligible for deportation to Colombia and possibly lead to his freedom.

Within weeks of sending that letter, Lehder was whisked away into the night, according to several federally protected witnesses at the Mesa Unit in Arizona where the authorities kept Lehder. No one saw Carlos Lehder for ten years.

Reliable law enforcement sources that I've talked with insist he's in the WITSEC, a witness protection program designed specifically to house federal prisoners. WITSEC inmates are usually put away from the general prison population for their own safety, say my law enforcement sources. In Lehder's case it's because of his testimony against General Noriega, they speculate.

Such prisoners rarely ever see the light of day again and are forbidden any outside contact. Break the rule and you can be thrown out of WITSEC and put back into the dangerous setting of the general prison population.

In the years during Lehder's disappearance, many other people, some of whom I have talked with and are not in law enforcement, insist that Lehder is out of prison and is most likely working for the U.S. government, possibly the U.S. Treasury or the CIA. Why? Lehder had knowledge of the drug trade and the contacts in the criminal world, they say.

I have met people in Colombia who claim to have seen Lehder in his hometown of Armenia where he has supposedly partied much like he did in his glory days. Other Colombians claim it is a fact that Lehder is living in Germany. Meanwhile, Crazy Charlie has become an urban legend in cyberspace with speculation abounding about his alleged connection to Mena, Arkansas, which claims a conspiracy involving murder, drugs and a President Bill Clinton administration cover up.

In 2005 Carlos Lehder appeared in a courtroom to challenge the terms of his imprisonment. In May 2007, Lehder's lawyers requested the Colombian Supreme Court to order the Colombian government to request his release from the United States because of the violations of his cooperation agreement. In early 2008 he briefly appeared in court again, fueling more speculation about the drug lord legend.

In early January 2015, one Colombian newspaper claimed that Lehder would be released soon and extradited to Germany. Other reports claim that Lehder is now in a minimum security prison with access to family, TV and even a computer with e-mail. Sources say, however, it is still impossible to reach Lehder.

As of this writing, Lehder is still in prison, no doubt still scheming to find a way to be free. Would he have access to the hundreds of millions, perhaps billions of dollars he made during his years as a drug kingpin? Most sources familiar with the drug trade doubt it. As George Jung explained, "That money is long gone."

Lehder would be 69 years old in 2016, still young enough that, with good health, he could enjoy a number of years of living if he managed to secure his freedom. But there is really nothing in it, at this point, for Uncle Sam to free the drug lord.

It's a good bet that Lehder has never publicly told everything he knows about the international drug trade. He probably still knows a lot about the CIA, Iran Contra, and successive U.S. presidencies from Richard Nixon to George Bush, Sr., that has never been made public and could embarrass the U.S. Besides, would Germany or Colombia really want someone living in their country who espouses the outlandish and Neo-Nazi views that Lehder has in the past and probably still does?

Is it really in the best interest of anyone in a position of power to set Lehder free to roam the world? I don't think so. After all, he is the man whom history has come to know as Crazy Charlie.

☙ ❧

UPDATE

Belisario Betancur Cuartas - President of Colombia from 1982 to 1986. He remains active in Latin American and international affairs.

Contras - The label given to the various rebel groups in opposition to the Sandinista Junta of National Reconstruction Government in Nicaragua. *The Contras* remained active until the early 1990s.

Pablo Escobar - Continued his war against the Colombian state after Lehder was sent to prison in 1988. On December 2, 1993, Colombian troops killed Escobar on a roof top in a middle class barrio of Medellín.

George Jung - Released from prison on June 2, 2014, after serving nearly twenty years for drug-smuggling. His life story was portrayed in the 2001 film *Blow*, starring Johnny Depp.

G. Gordon Liddy - Watergate conspirator imprisoned with Lehder at the federal prison in Danbury and served as a role model for him. Liddy was released in 1977 and became a popular radio talk show host. Liddy retired on July 27, 2012.

Robert Merkle - **T**he prosecutor in Lehder's 1988 trial, remained U.S. attorney for the Middle District of Florida until 1988 when he resigned. He then ran for U.S. Senate but lost. Merkle died of cancer on May 5, 2003.

Alfonso Lopez Michelsen - President of Colombia from 1974 to 1978 and an intermediary between the Colombian government and the Medellín Cartel, died on July 11, 2007 of a heart attack.

Yemel Nacel - Lehder's former wife, is dead.

General Manuel Noriega - Served as military dictator of Panama until 1989 when an invasion ousted him from power and made him a prisoner of war. Flown to the United States, Noriega was convicted of drug trafficking, racketeering, and money laundering in April 1992. After his U.S. prison sentence ended in September 2007, he was extradited to France in April 2010 where he served more time. Conditionally released on September 23, 2011, Noriega was extradited to Panama on December 11, 2011, where he is now serving a twenty-year sentence.

Fabio Ochoa - Extradited from Colombia to the U.S on drug trafficking charges in September 2001. Two years later, a U.S. court convicted him of trafficking, conspiracy and distribution of cocaine to the U.S. He was sentenced to thirty years in a U.S. federal prison· Ochoa is now in federal prison in Jesup, Georgia.

Jorge Ochoa - In September 1990, as the war between Escobar and the Colombian state raged, Colombian President *César Gaviria Trujillo* offered drug traffickers reduced prison sentences to be served in Colombia in an effort to entice them to surrender. Jorge Luis surrendered to the Colombian police in January 1991. He was released from Colombian prison in July 1996 after serving a five-and-a-half year prison sentence for drug trafficking.

Juan David Ochoa - Served five years in prison as a result of his plea bargain and was released in January 1996. On July 25, 2013, Ochoa died of a heart attack.

Lynden Pindling - Served as leader of the Bahamas' Progressive Liberal Party (PLP) until 1997 when he resigned from public life because of scandal. Pindling died on August 26, 2000.

Jose Quinon - One of Lehder's defense lawyers in his 1988 trial, still practices law in Miami.

Jack Carlton Reed - Was Carlos Lehder's co-defendant in their epic 1988 trial in Jacksonville. Reed was sentenced to two consecutive life terms and fined $2 million. He was incarcerated at the Federal Correctional Institute in Memphis, Tennessee, and later moved to a federal medical center. After spending nearly twenty-three years behind bars,

Reed was granted a clemency release, which reduced his sentence to time served. He died in prison on October 12, 2009.

Jose Gonzalo Rodriguez Gacha - Managed to stay free and on the run until December 15, 1989, when he was involved in a shootout with Colombian police. Rodríguez Gacha reportedly committed suicide by detonating a grenade on his face after watching his son get killed in the shootout.

Sandinistas (The Sandinista National Liberation Front or FSLN) **-** Lost the Nicaraguan election in 1990 to Violeta Barrios de Chamorro, but they retained a plurality of seats in the legislature. The FSLN remains one of Nicaragua's two leading parties.

Ed Shohat - One of Lehder's defense lawyers in his 1988 trial, still practices law in Miami.

Carlos Toro - Lehder's boyhood friend and later associate, became an undercover informant for the DEA soon after Lehder's trial and conviction.

Robert Vesco - The so-called fugitive financier, who was living in Cuba at the time of Lehder's trial. In 1996 Cuban authorities jailed Vesco for economic crimes they accusing him of committing in Cuba. But President Fidel Castro refused to extradite Vesco to the United States. Vesco died on November 23, 2007, in Havana, Cuba, at age 71.

Ed Ward – Who flew drug shipments to the U.S for Carlos Lehder, went into the Federal Witness Protection Program soon after testifying against Lehder.

Steve Yakovac - Testified in Carlos Lehder's 1988 trial, and then entered the Federal Witness Protection Program.

☙ ❧

ACKNOWLEDGEMENTS

I would like to thank all the people who helped make this book possible:

MayCay Beeler, George Jung, Mike McManus, Eileen O'Connor, Tom Tederington and Carlos Toro for allowing me to interview them and for sharing their thoughts and insights on the Carlos Lehder story.

Lew Rice, Todd Cimino, Jack Toal, and David G. Wilson for helping to arrange interviews.

Barbara Casey for editing the manuscript and providing valuable suggestions for its improvement.

The Dacus Library for granting printing and interlibrary loan privileges.

All the sources whom I've interviewed over the years and who have helped me broaden my understanding and knowledge of drug trafficking, Colombian history and the war on drugs.

My wife Magdalena for your love, support and encouragement through the years. Knowing you are there makes it worthwhile to get up each morning and grapple with the craft of writing.

☙ ❧

SELECTED BIBLIOGRAPHY

BOOKS

Beeler, MayCay. Buccaneer: The Provocative Odyssey of Jack Reed, Adventurer, Drug Smuggler and Pilot Extraordinaire, (Strategic Media Books, Rock Hill SC), 2014.

Bowden, Mark. Killing Pablo: The Hunt for the World's Greatest Outlaw, (Penguin Books, NY), 2002.

Chepesiuk, Ron. *Cali versus Escobar: The War of the Cartels*, (Strategic Media Books, Rock Hill, SC), 2014.

Drug Lords: The Rise and Fall of the Cali Cartel (Milo Books, Birmingham, UK), 2003.

Copperwaite, Paul. *The Mammoth Book of Drug Barons,* (Robinson, London), 2010.

Eddy, Paul and others. *The Cocaine Wars,* (W.W. Norton, New York), 1988.

Escobar, Roberto, *The Accountant's Story: Inside the Violent World of the Medellín Cartel* (Grand Central Publishing, New York), 2009.

Gugliotta, Guy, and Jeff Leen. Kings of Cocaine: Inside the Medellín Cartel: An Astonishing Story of Murder, Money and International Corruption (Simon and Shuster, New York), 1990.

Kemper, Frederick. Divorcing the Dictator: America's Bungled Affair with Noriega (Putnam, New York), 1990.

Kirkpatrick, Sidney, *Turning the Tide: One Man Against the Medellín Cartel* (Book Surge, New York), 2010.

Kline, Harvey F. *Historical Dictionary of Colombia,* (Scarecrow Press, New York), 2012.

Levenda, Peter. Unholy Alliance: A History of Nazi Involvement in the Occult, (Bloomsbury Academic, New York), 2002.

William Norris, *Snowbird: The Rise and Fall of a Medellín Drug Pilot,* (SnynergEbooks, New York), 2002.

Orozco, Jose Eliecer, El Hombre. Bogota, 1987.

Porter, Bruce. Blow: How a Small Town Boy Made a Million Dollars with Medellín Cartel and Lost It All, (St. Martin's Griffin, New York), 2014.

Rincon, Fabio. Intimidades del Caso Lehder, Bogota, 1987.

Scott, Dale. *Cocaine Politics: Drugs, Armies and the CIA in Central America,* (University of California Press, Berkeley, CA), 1998.

Streitfield, Donnie. *Cocaine: An Unauthorized Biography,* (Picador, London), 2003.

Strong, Simon. *Whitewash: Pablo Escobar and the Cocaine Wars,* (Pan Books, New York), 1995.

COURT RECORDS

U.S. Versus Carlos Enrique Lehder-Rivas AKA Joe Lehder, Court of Appeals for the Eleventh Circuit, Case No-88-3344, March 25, 1992.

U.S. Versus Lehder-Rivas No 81-82 Cr J—12, United States District Court, Florida, Jacksonville

Division, August 31, 1987.

MAGAZINE AND NEWSPAPER ARTICLES

"Bahamas Won't Let U.S. Seize Lehder's Property," *Times Wire Services,* May 22, 1988.

"Bail Denied for Reputed Cocaine Kingpin," *Toronto Star*, February 10, 1987.

"Cocaine Kingpins Flee Colombia," *Miami Herald*, September 18, 1983.

"Drug Baron on in U.S. Runs for Office," *Toronto Star*, February 4, 1988.

"Drug Lord: Funds Went to Contras," *Newsday,* November 26, 1991.

"Drug Lords Bought Noriega, Trial Told," *Toronto Star,* September 17, 1991.

"Drug Runners Banked Bags of Cash Deposited at Bank of Nova Scotia," *Toronto Star,* April 9, 1988.

"Drug Trafficker Links Fugitive to Laundering," *Knight Ridder News Service,* November 27, 1991.

"Former Cartel Kingpin Says Drug Leaders Gave Contras $20 Million," *Associated Press*, May 4, 1990.

"Testifying at Manuel Noriega's Drug Trial," *Newsday,* November 26, 1991.

Adams, Nathan, Cocaine Kings: A Study in Evil," *Reader's Digest*, December, 1988, p.230 plus

"U.S Can Confiscate Lehder's Bahamian Assets, Jury Rules, *Times Wire Service,* May 21, 1988.

"U.S. Offered to Okay Drug Dealing to Get Contra Aid, Smuggler Says," *Associated Press*, November 22, 1991.

Bleifuss, Joel, "The Scandal Behind the Scandal," *San Jose Mercury News*, April 14, 1989.

Gugliotta, Guy and Jeff Leen, "Drug Cartel's Carlos Lehder: Cocaine Lord Falls to Earth: Jury

Selection Enters Third Week in Trial of Key Figure," *Miami Herald,* October, 19, 1987.

Hanlon, Michael, "A Sting Avenged Barry Seal Used to Run Drugs for Fun and Profit," *Toronto Star,* March 29, 1986.

Jackson, Robert L, "Carter Leader Reveals Secrets of Drug World, *St. Petersburg Times,* November 21, 1991.

"Drug Lords Aided Contras, Kingpin Explained," *St. Petersburg Times,* November 26, 1991.

"Ex-Drug Kingpin Testifies Against Noriega," St. Petersburg Times, November 20, 1991.

Matthews, Geoffrey. "The Rise and Fall of the Legendary Carlitos - Carlos Lehder," *Times* (London, England) May 20, 1988.

Miller, Steve. "Boston George's Big Score," *Boston Magazine*, February 2015.

Moushey, Bill. "Once Carlos Lehder was atop the Most Wanted List," *Pittsburg Post-Gazette*, June 15, 1996.

Pardo, Alvaro. "Revenge Killings Feared After the Arrest of Drug Boss," *Sydney Morning Herald,* February 7, 1987.

Parry, Robert. "Contra-Cocaine was a Real Conspiracy," *Consortium News,* December 3, 2013.

Ross, Timothy. "Mania for Power Destroys Carlos—Carlos Lehder, Drug Dealer," *Sunday Times,* (London), May 22, 1988.

Rush Valerie. "Carlos Lehder Rivas: The Fall of an 'Untouchable,'" *EIR,* February 20, 1987.

Schiller, Bill. "Lehder Often Did Business in Toronto," *Toronto Star*, April 17, 1988.

Todd, David, "Evidence Grows that Contras Sold Drugs to Buy Weapons," *Toronto Star,* May 3, 1987.

INTERNET ARTICLES

"Hatred of All things Yankee Absorbs Lehder," *Times Wire Services,* May 19, 1988.

Ames, Justin. "Norman's Cay and Carlos Lehder," *The Velvet Rocket*, December 2007 and February

2008, http:thevelvetrocket.com. Frontline, Interview, Drug Wars, "Carlos Toro," www.pbs.org.

"Fernando Arenas," www.pbs.org.

"George Jung," www.pbs.org.

"Jorge Ochoa," www.pbs.org.

Ruppert, Michael. "FTW Special Investigation, Carlos Lehder," Multi-Part Series, 2001,

www.fromthewilderness.com.

Smith, Larry. "Carlos Lehder's Bahamian Legacy," www.bahamapundit.com, July 19, 2006.

ଓ ଃ

INDEX

Air Montes Company Ltd 54
Alfonso Lopez Michelsen 81, 152
Alphonso Lopez Michelsen 100
Arbron Miami International Distributor Inc 68
Armenia 8, 10, 14, 17, 53, 54, 55, 56, 58, 62, 63, 67, 81, 82, 110, 148
Bahamas . 17, 31, 32, 33, 37, 38, 44, 47, 48, 50, 54, 57, 128, 129, 136, 153, 161
Barry Kane 30, 32
Barry Seale 105
Belisario Betancur..... iv, 61, 76, 90, 151
Bella Vista 31, 32
Bernardo Antonio Vasquez 107
Berrigan brothers 22
Betsy Strautman 29
Bishop Dario Castrillon...................... 57
Cano Izaza 118, 119
Caqueta 68
Carlos Enrique 17, 161
Carlos Jiminez Gomez 102
Carlos Lehder iii, iv, 8, 9, 10, 11, 12, 22, 35, 43, 49, 53, 56, 62, 70, 73, 80, 81, 84, 85, 106, 110, 111, 113, 121, 143, 147, 148, 153, 155, 157, 163, 164, 165
Carlos Lipher 17
Carlos Toro.... 9, 10, 35, 39, 90, 94, 105, 106, 123, 154, 157, 164
Charles Beckwith 39
CIA Director William Casey 96
Citizens against Crime 74
Clifford Irving 22
Club America 10
Colombia .. iii, iv, v, 8, 10, 11, 14, 25, 26, 28, 31, 32, 35, 39, 44, 45, 46, 50, 52, 53, 58, 59, 63, 64, 66, 67, 71, 72, 75, 76, 77, 78, 80, 81, 93, 94, 97, 99, 100, 101, 102, 105, 106, 107, 109, 110, 111, 112, 114, 115, 116, 117, 118, 119, 128, 133, 135, 142, 143,145, 147, 148, 149, 151, 152, 153, 160, 162
Colombia Palace of Justice 115
Colombian Defense Ministry 118
Crazy Charliev, 8, 12, 15, 17, 35, 53, 67, 69, 72, 94, 112, 113, 123, 132, 143, 144, 148, 149
Cuba 35, 50, 64, 103, 104, 111, 144, 154
Danbury Correctional Institute 19
Danbury prison 13, 21
Death to the Kidnappers 64
Don Pablo 60
Eben Mann 136
Ed Shohat 126, 154
Ed Ward 41, 42, 72, 155
Edwin Meese 144
Elizabeth Rivas 9
Enrique Parejo Gonzalez 119
Envigado 61
Fabio Ochoa, Sr 44, 45
Fernando Arenas 13, 43, 164
Fidel Castro .. 50, 87, 102, 134, 145, 154
Fourth Estate 57, 118
Francis Mullen 144
Frank Shea 29, 30
Fred Lehder 97
G. Gordon Liddy 22, 28, 151

General Manuel Noriega ... 49, 94, 141, 146, 152
General Omar Torrijos 96
George Jung.. 16, 19, 22, 28, 38, 42, 86, 132, 133, 149, 151, 157, 164
George Schultz 100
Griselda Blanco 71
Hacienda Abundancia 113
Howard W. Melton 129
Ivan Dario Guizado 78
Jack Reed 41, 42, 130, 159
Jaime Michelsen Uribe 81
Jairo Ortega 61
James Smith 73
Joe Kennedy 18
Joe Leather 17
Joe Lehder 16, 161
Joe Lemon 17
Johnny Depp 23, 151
Jorge Ochoaiv, 38, 43, 69, 88, 100, 101, 102, 103, 106, 107, 110, 114, 153, 165
Jose Gonzalo Rodriguez Gacha ....iv, 44, 46, 102, 154
Jose Quinon 126, 153
Jung .. 15, 16, 22, 23, 24, 25, 26, 27, 28, 29, 30, 31, 32, 33, 38, 42, 49, 72, 132, 133, 134, 135
La Posada Alemana..........55, 57, 62, 82
Lara Bonilla .... iv, 61, 62, 76, 77, 78, 79, 80, 81, 100, 101, 102, 112
Latin Nationalist Movement 109
Lehder. iv, v, 8, 9, 10, 11, 12, 13, 14, 15, 16, 17, 18, 19, 21, 22, 25, 26, 27, 28, 29, 30, 31, 32, 33, 34, 35, 37, 38, 39, 40, 41, 42, 43, 44, 45, 46, 47, 48, 49, 50, 51, 52, 53, 54, 55, 56, 57, 58, 59, 61, 62, 63, 64, 66, 67, 71, 72, 73, 75, 76, 77, 79, 81, 82, 93, 94, 97, 98, 101, 103, 104, 105, 106, 107, 109, 111, 112, 113, 114, 119, 120, 121, 122, 123, 124, 125, 126, 127, 128, 129, 130, 131, 132, 133, 134, 135, 136, 137, 139, 140, 141, 143, 144, 145, 146, 147, 148, 149, 151, 152, 153, 154, 155, 160, 161, 162, 164
Lewis Tambs 75, 78
Lilianna Garcia Osirio 17
Lopez Michelsen 100, 101, 102
Luis Carlos Quintero-Cruz 107
Luis Fernando Mejia 56
Lynden Pindling 49, 50, 51, 153
M-19 ....63, 64, 65, 66, 112, 115
Manizales 9, 11
Marta Ochoa 142
MAS 64, 65, 66, 67
Medellín.....iii, iv, 12, 28, 31, 40, 43, 44, 45, 46, 47, 48, 53, 54, 59, 60, 61, 62, 63, 66, 67, 69, 70, 71, 74, 75, 76, 77, 78, 79, 81, 93, 94, 98, 99, 100, 101, 102, 103, 104, 105, 106, 107, 109, 110, 111, 114, 115, 116, 117, 118, 119, 122, 123, 124, 140, 142, 145,151, 152, 160
Medlin Cartel iii
Meta 114
Miguel Velez 107
MLN 109
Movimiento Latino 82
Nicaragua... iv, 35, 47, 94, 97, 103, 104, 106, 151, 154
Nicolas Barletta 99
Nigel Bowe 50
Norman Bailey 96
Norman's Cay17, 32, 34, 35, 37, 38, 39, 40, 41, 43, 44, 47, 49, 50, 51, 52, 53, 72, 75, 105, 106, 129, 130, 164
Operation Raccoon 52
Pablo Escobar iv, 31, 38, 44, 45, 46, 59, 60, 62, 77, 80, 89, 105, 106, 109, 122, 128, 151, 161
Panama Canal 44, 96, 97

Peace Corps 18
Police Major William Lemus 121
Prohibition 18, 59
Puerta Vallarta, Mexico 24
Quindio 54, 55, 56, 57, 109
Ranch of the Abundance................ 113
Raul Castro..................................... 104
Richard Barile.................................. 23
Richard James Barile 141
Richard Novak.................................. 40
Ring Lardner, Jr 21
Rivas Carlos..................................... 17
Rivas Enrique 17
Robert Merkle................ 127, 144, 152
Robert Vesco..48, 49, 86, 135, 136, 154
Rodrigo Arenas Bentacur 55
Rodrigo Lara Bonilla..iii, 61, 76, 89, 119
Roselio Cessinica 17
Roselio de Grullaid 17
Ruben Montes 17
Russ O'Hara.................................... 136
Sandinistas...94, 97, 104, 106, 145, 154
South Florida Task Force 74
Stephen Yakovac.............................. 31
Toro.....9, 10, 11, 12, 13, 14, 15, 35, 42, 47, 48, 51, 64, 95, 105, 106, 123, 124
Tranquilandia 68, 69, 70, 77, 117
U.S. Drug Enforcement Administration 117
Walter Cronkite................................. 40
Wilhelm Lehder.................................. 9
William Bedoya 76
Winny Polly 29
Yakovac......31, 32, 33, 34, 72, 135, 155
Yemel Nacel 15, 135, 140, 152

ଔ ଷ ଔ ଷ